ADVANCE PRAISE FOR

RE-ROUTED: THE PAIN, PURPOSE, AND PEOPLE THAT MADE ME A LEADER

"*Re-Routed* is a practical, encouraging 'love letter' to leaders and would-be leaders. Mike's authenticity, passion, and years of experience leading hand-in-hand with people shine through. The 4 Disciplines are simple and actionable for growth and influence—anywhere—not just when one gets re-routed."

— **Jon Kidwell,** CEO, Lead*well*
Author, *Redefine Your Servant Leadership*

"Mike Brown wrote a leadership book for the true leader—one who knows difficulties, challenges, imperfections, and struggles. His candor and passion inspire and he shoots from the hip and from the heart. Mike's years of personal experience and impressive history give the reader a hard-won gift—self acceptance and healing."

— **Michelle Auerbach,** President Modaka Communications,
Author *The Life-Saving Skill of Story*

"*Re-Routed* is filled with life, leadership, and the highs and lows that come with both. Mike shares his journey with honesty, vulnerability, and authenticity, offering genuine inspiration along the way. It paints a powerful picture of life and leadership in all their complexity and depth."

— **Brent Pentenburg**, Friend and Colleague

RE-ROUTED

The Pain, Purpose, and People That Made Me a Leader

Mike Brown, Jr.

LUMINOUS MOON PRESS
BOULDER, CO

Published by Luminous Moon Press, LLC, Boulder, CO
luminousmoon.com

First Edition: March 2026

ISBN: 978-1-970573-01-5 (Paperback)
ISBN: 978-1-970573-02-2 (Hardcover)
ISBN: 978-1-970573-03-9 (eBook)

Publisher's Cataloging-in-Publication
(Provided by Cassidy Cataloguing Services, Inc.)

Names: Brown, Mike (Michael Eugene), 1973- author.
Title: Re-routed : the pain, purpose, and people that made me a leader / Mike Brown, Jr.
Description: Boulder, CO : Luminous Moon Press, [2026]
Identifiers: ISBN: 9781970573015 (paperback) | 9781970573022 (hardcover) | 9781970573039 (ebook)
Subjects: LCSH: Brown, Mike (Michael Eugene), 1973- | Businesspeople. | Leadership--Religious aspects--Christianity. | Management--Religious aspects--Christianity. | Decision making. | Business communication. | Christian life. | Loss (Psychology) | LCGFT: Autobiographies. | BISAC: BUSINESS & ECONOMICS / Leadership. | BUSINESS & ECONOMICS / Human Resources & Personnel Management. | RELIGION / Christian Ministry / Pastoral Resources.
Classification: LCC: BV4597.53.L43 B76 2026 | DDC: 206.1--dc23

Printed and bound in the United States of America

RE-ROUTED

The Pain, Purpose, and People That Made Me a Leader

CONTENTS

DEDICATION

To the broken and the brave, to the leaders who never saw themselves as such, but kept showing up anyway.

To the ones who were told they'd never make it, but did. To the ones still trying to believe they're enough.

To my late wife, Laura, whose grace, faith, and quiet strength held me up through some of the hardest storms of my life. Your memory is in every line of this book. Your legacy lives on in the love we built and the family we raised.

To my wife, Stacy, whose laughter, resilience, and fierce love gave me new life when I thought my story was over. You walked into the wreckage with me and chose to stay. You are God's reminder that restoration is real.

To my children Robbie, Kevin, Hayden, Abbie, Colby, and Wyatt, my reasons, my teachers, and my pride. Some of you were born into my arms, others walked into my life later, but all of you are part of my heart. I've failed you at times. I've tried my best. I hope you know that every hard decision, every late-night prayer, and every lesson I've tried to live by was for you.

To my dad and stepmom, and to every member of our family who was there when I needed to find myself, thank you. Thank you for taking me in and helping reset my life.

To my mom, sister, grandmother, and every member of my family who held me up when I couldn't stand on my own, thank you for staying. Even in the mess. Even when we didn't get it right.

To those I've hurt, misunderstood, or failed along the way: I'm sorry. This book is part of my healing, and I hope, in some way, it helps yours too.

To the teenagers in the back row of retreats, who didn't want to sing, but found their voice anyway.

To the Trinity Youth crew, who proved that worship is leadership, and that mission can be built with a microphone and a message. You reminded me that passion is powerful when it's real.

To Dave, Gigi, Lance, David, Robbie, Brent, Andre and Jon, thank you for modeling strength, wisdom, faith, and grace, and for walking beside me as God shaped both the leader and the man I am becoming.

To the Marlowe family: Mike, Melody, Cody, and Katie, your friendship, honesty, and willingness to walk with me through real conversations have guided me more than you know.

To every staff member, volunteer, and leader who's ever sat in a meeting with me, struggled under my leadership, grown through it, or helped me grow, you are part of this. Every success, every turning point, every breakthrough.

To the YMCA and Trinity United Methodist Church, a movement that gave me purpose, a platform, and people to love. Thank you for shaping me into a leader not just of programs, but of people.

To the abused, the addicted, the abandoned, I see you. I was you. This book is for you.

And to God, whom I have wrestled with, run from, cursed at, clung to, and ultimately surrendered to, thank you for never letting go, even when I did.

This is not just a leadership book.

It's a love letter to resilience.

It's a confession. A commission.

And a prayer:

That we would all lead with more heart and love with more truth.

— Mike

ACKNOWLEDGMENT

This book has been years in the making, shaped by moments of loss, love, faith, and leadership, but the title Re-Routed came from something much simpler: a conversation in the kitchen.

One night, while talking with my bonus son Wyatt about life, relationships, and choices, we landed on a powerful truth that sometimes God puts an answer right in front of us, and we still turn the other way. Not because we don't care, but because we're human. When we do, God, full of grace and patience, re-routes us. That moment reminded me of something I used to preach to teenagers as a youth pastor: that God's leadership is like a GPS. You might miss a turn, but He never gives up on getting you to your destination.

To the many leaders, friends, and colleagues I've served with across cities and seasons, thank you. Whether in youth ministry, boardrooms, or broken systems, your courage, collaboration, and commitment to people shaped the lessons in these pages.

To those who challenged me, inspired me, and sharpened me, your impact lives here.

To every person God placed in my life who offered purpose, opportunity, and grace; thank you for giving a young man with pain in his past a voice that mattered.

And to every reader walking through your own re-routing, I pray this book helps you see that detours aren't disqualifications. They're just divine redirections.

*You don't need
more strategy.*

*You need
more heart.*

INTRODUCTION

LEADING WITH LOVE WHEN THE WORLD NEEDS IT MOST

I've never written a book before, but I've lived one. Every page, every chapter, has been written with tears, grit, hope, and redemption. Some people spend their entire lives climbing ladders, only to realize they leaned them against the wrong wall. Me? I spent decades building a ladder from scratch, out of broken wood, rope I braided myself, and whatever nails I could find, only to have it knocked over, time and again. Somehow, by God's grace, I kept rebuilding.

This book is not for perfect people. If you've had every opportunity handed to you, if your life has gone according to plan, if leadership has been smooth and free of heartbreak, then this book might confuse you. If you've ever been rerouted, if you've had to start over, been crushed by loss, doubted your worth, or questioned your calling, then this book is for you. If you've ever led people who didn't believe in you, loved people who couldn't love you back, or stayed faithful when it would've been easier to walk away, then I hope you find yourself in these pages.

Re-Routed is not just the story of how I became a leader. It's the story of how God used detours, breakdowns, heartbreaks, and miracles to shape a calling far greater than I ever imagined. It's the story of a boy from broken places who became a man committed to building healing places, a leader shaped not by titles or degrees, but by trauma, tenacity, and trust.

I'm writing this for every person who's ever thought they missed their turn. For every leader who's had to take the long way around. For every father who's had to find healing while still holding his family together. For every CEO who's had to smile through disappointment. For every believer who's screamed into the void, "God, are you sure this is the plan?"

Over the course of 34 years with a wonderful organization, I've led in six different states, worked with thousands of staff, raised over half a billion dollars, and helped build programs, camps, and community centers. None of that matters as much as this: I survived. Not just physically; I survived spiritually, emotionally, and relationally. I didn't give up, and that, more than any title, award, or accomplishment, is what leadership truly is: not perfection, but perseverance. Not dominance, but devotion. Not having all the answers, but knowing how to ask better questions.

You'll meet my family in these pages, those who made me and those I've made. You'll see my scars. You'll feel my failures. You'll walk with me through the grief of losing my son, Nathaniel Wyatt, at birth. You'll hear about my wife, Laura, who fought cancer with the same grace she raised our children, and who I buried far too soon. You'll witness how, even in the valley of death and despair, God rerouted me toward life.

The GPS metaphor runs deep in my story. I've taken wrong turns. I've ignored the voice trying to guide me. Just when I thought I was lost, that calm, reassuring voice said again: "Recalculating." That's the mercy of God, no matter how far off course you go, He can always reroute you.

This book is a leadership roadmap, yes, but it's also a love letter to redemption. A blueprint for those who lead with heart, not just strategy. A guide for how to build culture, community, and character when the world feels cold and transactional. A declaration that love and kindness are not soft; they are strong. They are what outlast titles, trends, and turmoil.

If you're still reading, you're probably one of my people. You believe leadership is sacred. You know pain can be a teacher. You've chosen to love, even when it would be easier to quit. So let's begin. Not at the start, but somewhere in the middle. Where real stories unfold, and real leaders rise.

Over the last three decades, I've come to believe that every truly transformational leader embodies four principles: ***Teachability,*** the willingness to grow and be shaped; ***Initiative,*** the courage to move when others hesitate;

Discipline, the grit to stay the course when it would be easier to quit; and ***Passion,*** the heartbeat that fuels mission and anchors us to people. These are more than traits; they are truths I've lived. They've walked with me through funerals, through failure, through second chances I didn't deserve. They've helped me become a leader who doesn't just build organizations, but who builds people.

None of those principles mean anything without ***love***. Love is the thread that ties them all together. Love is the force that keeps a leader humble enough to learn, bold enough to act, focused enough to persist, and tender enough to care deeply. Without love, leadership becomes noise. With it, leadership becomes legacy.

This book is for the leader who's tired. For the one who feels invisible. For the executive who's questioning their purpose, and the frontline worker who doesn't feel seen. It's for the person who knows what it's like to lead with a broken heart and still believe in healing.

If you've ever wondered if what you do matters, if who you are is enough, then I want you to know this: your story isn't over. Your leadership isn't disqualified. Your impact may be deeper than you'll ever realize.

This is your invitation. To lead with heart. To lead with courage. Above all, to lead with love.

WHAT THE MIRROR REVEALED

Looking back on my journey, I don't see perfection. I see grace. I see re-routing. I see the hand of God, not always in the rescue, but in the redirection. I see those who hurt me and those who healed me. I see the moments I nearly gave up, and the miracles that kept me moving forward.

I've held many titles in my life: son, counselor, CEO, youth pastor, husband, widower, father. But the most important one? Survivor. Because despite everything, I survived. By the grace of faith, the gift of others, and a strength I didn't know I had, I began to live again.

But leadership? Leadership isn't about surviving. It's about transformation.

That's what this book is about. It's about the lessons I've learned, not just from boardrooms and budgets, but from hospital rooms and heartbreaks. From staff retreats to suicide attempts. From adoption and abandonment. From knowing what it's like to lead with power and what it feels like to have none.

Leadership isn't about surviving.

It's about transformation.

This book is not a "how-to." It's a "why-to." A "who-with." A "what-now."
Because you don't need more strategy, you need more heart.
And that's what I hope to offer.

TURNING THE PAGE

Now that you know where I've come from, let's talk about what I've learned. The principles that carried me. The values that sustained me. The truths that still guide me when I'm not sure what to do next.

These next chapters aren't theories. They're battle-tested beliefs that changed my life—and I believe they can change yours too.

Let's begin with the first of the four: **Teachability**.

REFLECTION QUESTIONS

- When you look back at your own story, what moments shaped you the most, and why?
- Who are the people who believed in you when you didn't believe in yourself?
- What pain are you still carrying that might be part of your re-routing, not your disqualification?
- Have you ever been in a season where you felt lost or forgotten? How did you find your way out—or are you still finding it?
- What does "starting over" look like in your life right now? What might God be preparing you for through it?

It's not the know-it-alls who lead change; it's the learn-it-alls who do.

chapter one

TEACHABILITY
THE CAPACITY TO LEARN

"Leadership isn't about arriving—it's about becoming."

THE FOUNDATION OF GROWTH

Teachability is not a leadership buzzword. It's the soil from which all real growth emerges. It doesn't matter how many degrees you hold, how much influence you've gained, or how sharp your skills are, if you lose the willingness to learn, you've stopped leading.

The best leaders I've worked with weren't always the most charismatic or credentialed. They were the most teachable. They stayed curious. They invited feedback. They leaned into challenges without becoming defensive. They understood something vital: leadership is a journey, not a destination.

It was the Vice President for Program Services in Houston, Gigi, who first demonstrated to me the importance of teachability. I was a young program director. I had just moved to Houston. Gigi was one of those people who took interest in folks and had the passion about growing new leaders. Gigi was also the training and development person for the association. I had to go through all the certification classes with Gigi to learn how to lead, how to teach in front of people, how to give trainer of Trainer Courses, how to be on stage and talk to folks when you're training.

Gigi taught me that I didn't know everything, but she taught me in a gentle way by showing that she knew she didn't know everything. She was willing to listen to and learn from everyone around her, even the 24-year-old who thought he knew it all. She honored different perspectives and her willingness to learn made the room feel safe. She encouraged us to speak up and challenge her way of thinking and that helped me to do the same, even when my supervisors were in the room.

Her biggest gift to me was that she didn't always have to be the one leading. Gigi would call on us to lead. She would let us be the voice in the room. She would put you in front of 100 people to lead, and then she would learn from you. I did not yet have the confidence, but her attitude of teachability helped me see that I could contribute.

Teachability kept me moving when confidence failed me. It helped me launch successful programs in areas I initially knew nothing about, such as youth sports. I wasn't athletic growing up. I didn't understand the rules the way others did. Because of Gigi, I didn't pretend to know. I asked for help. I brought in skilled volunteers. I listened to people who knew more than I did. I came to understand the idea that "If you're not learning, you're irrelevant." So my programs thrived, not because I had all the answers, but because I asked the right questions.

One of the things I learned from Gigi was never to be afraid to ask for help and never to be afraid to learn. I've been a lifelong learner, even in moments, that I know that I'm the problem. A great example is when I took over a massive youth sports program, and I knew nothing about the sport. I didn't play sports. I didn't follow sports. Still, I was the one who needed to organize the basketball season. I took the 400 registrations, I threw them on the ground, I divided them by ages, and I made the teams. I published the teams. I thought I needed to put my effort into the kick-off for the program so I went all out. It was my best work. I had balloons, I set up a stage in the middle of the courts, It was decorated. Parents were mesmerized at how I turned sports into amazing fun.

Then the teams started playing. I knew nothing about team sports, so it was a mess. I built the teams based on age, but not skill. There were some teams with incredible players and some that were all weaker players. So as the first round of games went on, you had one team that was just squashing the other team. There were little kids crying because they couldn't score. The same parents who loved my opener were now frustrated. I could see it was a disaster, so I had the humility to call it. I got on the microphone, I had all the officials blow their whistles, and I called the gym to order. There were

200 people staring at me while I admitted I was the problem. I said, "Folks I have done the best that I know how, but I can't allow us to go through eight weeks of this program the way that I've organized it. So, as of now, it's canceled, and what I need from all of you is to bring your jerseys back, and I need those coaches and parents who have a love for basketball and know the sport to help me reassess these teams, get us back on track, and in two weeks, we're going to start this program the right way, so that every kid is successful."

About 80% of the gym clapped and people came by and said, "That took guts." I said, "If you want a refund, I understand." Ten people took a refund, and eight of them came back. What I did next was learn from the parents. I had moms and grandparents helping fold shirts and redo packets. I had parents sit there and look at the forms and show me how to read the registration and explain the reason why there's a skill level on the registration. They helped me learn how to put the kids on teams appropriately, how to transfer a player if they were on a team that they shouldn't have been on, and all the necessary skills I lacked.

We reorganized and launched it two weeks later. That program, over the next two years, doubled, not because I knew it all, but because I was teachable. I came to see that I did not need to be the one in charge. It was a misconception I had had all my life—that I had to do it myself. There were so many lessons in that failure. One was to get and stay teachable. Also, that teachability means I had to learn to listen, adjust, and fail forward. If I did all that, I would not only raise my own potential, but I would combine the wisdom of all the people whose ideas I was willing to learn from and put to work.

That's the quiet power of teachability: it multiplies what you can do through the wisdom of others.

CHOOSING HUMILITY OVER EGO

Teachable leaders understand a critical truth: they don't have all the answers and they don't need to.

When I was promoted to full-time at nineteen years old in Visalia, California, I wasn't the most experienced. I wasn't the most polished. But I was humble. My boss, Dave, didn't choose me because I had it all figured out. He chose me because I was coachable.

I listened.
I adjusted.
I tried.
I failed forward.

I absorbed everything I could from the people around me, people who had been doing the work longer and better than I had. That humility became the backbone of my growth.

Leadership, over time, tempts us to forget that.

Titles. Promotions. Praise. They whisper: *You've arrived.*

But that's a lie.

The moment you stop learning is the moment you start declining. Ego will always sabotage potential. Humility protects it.

And humility says, *"I still have room to grow."*

CLOSED MINDSET

Influence

TEACHABLE MINDSET

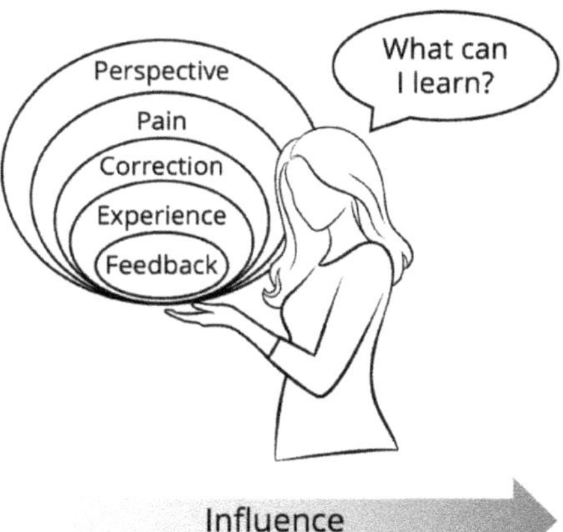

Influence

Influence expands in proportion to humility.

LEARNING FROM EVERY VOICE

Teachability requires more than just a willingness to listen, it requires the courage to listen beyond our comfort zones.

Some of the most profound lessons in my life didn't come from professors or high-level executives. They came from unexpected voices:

- Teenagers in our youth programs
- Part-time staff members
- Single moms navigating life with grit and grace in our after-school programs

I've learned more in locker rooms and staff lounges than in any formal classroom. Why? Because teachable leaders don't just absorb lessons from authority, they stay open to wisdom wherever it emerges.

LESSONS ARE EVERYWHERE

As a young director, I began to understand that teachability wasn't just about learning from those above me. It was about noticing what was happening around me.

When I stopped talking and started observing, something powerful happened: People started teaching me, without even knowing it.

- A volunteer's frustration would reveal a blind spot in our system.
- A child's innocent question would expose a gap in my own understanding.
- A staff member's body language would highlight misalignment in our team dynamics.

Every interaction became an opportunity to grow. When we stay open, the world becomes a classroom.

THE COURAGE TO BE WRONG

Teachable leaders aren't afraid to fail. They know that mistakes are often the best teachers and they don't waste time trying to pretend they got it right when they didn't. I've made hires I regretted, launched initiatives that flopped, and missed moments when I should have slowed down and listened. Those weren't wasted experiences. They were classrooms. They only became valuable when I had the courage to say, "I got that wrong. Let's try again."

One of my proudest leadership moments wasn't about success it was about how we responded to failure. A high-level leader on my team once made a mistake that cost us nearly a million dollars in grant money that we needed to function. It was a small error that snowballed into a big problem for the organization. The person who made the error took responsibility for the mistake and was willing and eager to sit down and make adjustments and learn from it. I was then able to take responsibility for my part and see how I had not understood everything at the beginning, maybe because I was not listening, and we both worked together to address the very expensive problem. We confronted it, learned from it, and moved through it together. That kind of honesty builds trust. That kind of courage builds culture. Because failure isn't the opposite of success, it's the pathway to it.

What we did was psychologically difficult. Often, we get hijacked with our feelings and we stop listening. We respond to what we think we heard or we are just unwilling to hear at all. I see myself do this with my kids sometimes, but it happens in work settings, too. My kids are trying to tell me something, but they can't get it out right, and I respond too quickly, and I don't hear the whole story, and I immediately react, and I fail in the way that I treated them or spoke to them, or the way that I made them feel. I know I am going too fast, not listening, or feeling too much, but I'm hijacked.

Later, and this is the lesson for me, I have to go back to them and own my mistake. Tell them I responded wrong. This just happened. The boys were watching the house and the dog while we were on vacation and our dog, who's only a year old, ate their pre-workout pills. That was about ten times the amount of caffeine a dog can handle. They called me, and while I tried to listen, I also responded out of fear. All they were trying to do is take responsibility for the situation and ask me what doctor they should take the dog to. Instead, out of fear and not listening to the fact that they were scared too, I got mad. What they needed me to do was help them navigate a difficult situation and they were being teachable, but I was not. I had to go back and apologize and recognize my contribution to the problem before we could make a solution together.

CONSISTENCY OVER COMFORT

Teachability isn't a seasonal trait. It has to be consistent, even when it's uncomfortable. It's easy to be open to feedback when you feel energized and affirmed. Can you still be teachable when you're tired? When are you frustrated? When someone challenges you in front of others?

True teachability shows up in the hard moments, in the tension, in the misunderstandings, in the uncomfortable truths. It shows up when a staff member tells you something you didn't want to hear, or when a peer offers a better idea than yours. It shows up when your kids call you out on something you preach but don't practice. It's in those moments that our growth is forged.

TEACHABILITY AND FAITH

Even my faith journey has been shaped by this principle. There have been seasons when I thought I had it all figured out, when my faith felt strong and certain. It was in the seasons of doubt, anger, and pain that I truly began to learn. When I lost my son. When I lost my wife. When I lost my sense of direction, it was in those moments that God gently reminded me: I am still teaching you. Even now, I remain a student of life, of leadership, and of love.

TEACHABILITY IS A DECISION

Every day, we face a choice: we can choose to be defensive or curious, to double down or to lean in, to pretend we have it all together, or to grow. Leadership is not about being right; it's about getting better. Getting better requires a posture of teachability. No matter how long we've been doing the work or how far we've come, there is always more to learn and more to become. That's what makes leadership so powerful, not that we've mastered the journey, but that we remain willing to keep taking the next step.

LESSONS FROM THE FIELD

Over the course of my thirty-plus years of leadership, I've had the privilege of working with thousands of staff, from brand-new part-timers to seasoned executives. If there's one thing I've seen time and time again, it's this: the people who thrive aren't always the ones with the most talent.

They're the ones with the most hunger. They walk into a training session with a notebook and a willingness to learn and grow. They don't let their experience harden them into rigidity. Instead, they let every role, every challenge, and every moment of feedback sharpen them into stronger leaders.

Teachability isn't just about listening, it's about **leaning in**. It's a posture of curiosity that shows up in both big and small moments. I've seen leaders succeed not because they had the flashiest resumes, but because they were intentional about learning from every opportunity. They asked questions in staff meetings. They reviewed their mistakes instead of defending them. They treated every team member as a potential teacher, no matter their position. Because of that, they didn't just grow in skill, they grew in character.

You don't have to know everything to lead well, you just have to know how to learn. When I let go of the pressure to be the smartest or most qualified, I could focus on what truly mattered: creating a high-quality experience, serving families well, and building trust through transparency. In the process, I earned credibility, not by flexing expertise I didn't have, but by demonstrating that I was willing to grow into the leader my team deserved.

In every city I've led, whether in California, Texas, Georgia, Illinois or New York, this truth has remained constant: teachability is the great equalizer. It doesn't matter where you start, what you lack, or who doubts you. If you're willing to learn, you will rise. While others may coast on what they already know, you'll be building something stronger from what you're still learning. It's not the know-it-alls who lead change; it's the learn-it-alls who do.

FAILURE IS A BETTER TEACHER THAN SUCCESS

Some of my greatest failures weren't in a boardroom or on a stage, they were in the quiet places of my life. In my relationships. In the places where titles didn't matter, but love did. I've failed as a son, a boyfriend, a husband, a father, and a friend. For too long, I didn't want to admit that.

As a son, I lived in my own world.

Before I ever stood on a stage, led a team, or inspired others with stories of leadership, I was a boy who didn't feel seen. Born in Visalia, California, my childhood was defined not only by moments of love and laughter but also by a quiet pain; a kind of weight you carry without always realizing how heavy it is. It wasn't the kind of pain that makes headlines or sparks courtroom drama. No, this was the invisible kind, the kind that comes from being the odd one out.

I was a kid of divorce. I grew up in homes where men shouted more than they showed up. Where stepfathers either hurt my mom or ignored me completely. Where ridicule was a regular visitor, and kindness felt like a rare, distant memory.

I was shy. Uncertain. Different. I didn't have my parents' talents or confidence, and I often felt like I didn't belong anywhere. I was the tag-along, the kid who was tolerated at best, or sometimes the target. I was the one left behind, the one who didn't get the invite, who wore the wrong clothes, and who sat in the back of the class because the front felt too exposed.

When you're a child already weighed down by insecurity, being hurt by others seems inevitable. I was taken advantage of. Abused. Not once, but in moments that still sting, even now. It wasn't by family, it was by people who preyed on silence, who saw a boy too afraid to speak.

Even at school, I couldn't catch a break. Learning felt like a mountain I couldn't climb. I was often placed in lower academic tracks, not because I couldn't learn, but because I believed I couldn't. And worse, others believed it too. My clothes weren't brand-name. My shoes weren't fresh. My confidence? It didn't exist.

I ran cross-country because running made me feel free, like I could escape. Even then, there was no one cheering me on. My family was busy working, distracted, just trying to get by. I didn't blame them. I noticed. I always noticed.

My mother was suffering, too. I saw my mother's pain but didn't understand it. I felt the weight of helping to raise my siblings, but I never stopped to ask why things were so hard for her. I carried resentment instead of compassion. I judged instead of understanding. I didn't see her as a woman doing the best she could, I saw her through the narrow lens of my unmet needs. I've carried the guilt of that misunderstanding for a long time.

THE MOMENT I ALMOST DIDN'T MAKE IT

By seventeen, the pain I carried turned inward. I didn't want to live. I didn't see the point. When I did reach out to friends, to adults, to anyone who might listen, I was brushed off, told I just wanted attention. So I took that pain and turned it into a plan. I attempted suicide. By some miracle,

I survived. Not because I believed I should, but because God, even then, had a reroute in mind.

The hospital stay was isolating. The therapy was impersonal. I didn't talk much. I didn't trust. My mom was angry, confused, maybe even ashamed. My dad and stepmom flew in. For the first time, it felt like people noticed. Even then, it felt temporary. Like a moment of attention that would quickly fade. When I was finally released, it was a counselor, not a family member, who truly heard me. Who helped me transition? Who arranged for me to move back to California and live with my dad and stepmom? It wasn't perfect, but it was the beginning of something new.

CALIFORNIA ROOTS AND A REBIRTH

When I moved back to California after my suicide attempt, my father and stepmother took me in. I was seventeen, broken, and trying to rebuild my life from the inside out. It was the first time I had ever lived with them, the first child in their home and I had to learn everything from scratch. A new home. New expectations. A new rhythm of family life. I had to relearn how to trust, how to speak without fear, how to find comfort in simply being near my dad. For the first time, I felt like I had a chance to heal, to belong. That season of hope quickly turned confusing. Within a year, they adopted three young children and just like that, I didn't feel like a son anymore. I felt like a placeholder. The one who was too old, too wounded, too much. I was expected to help, to adjust, to make room. Emotionally, I had nothing left to give. I felt replaced, and the weight of it was more than I could carry.

At the time, I thought I was abandoned again. Now, I realize I was being redirected, re-routed toward something that would change my life. It's taken me years and a lot of painful growth to realize that season wasn't about rejection. It was about redirection. My father and stepmother didn't mean to replace me; they were building the family they felt called to create. As a hurting teenager, I couldn't see that. I saw it through the lens of my own pain: not enough, too broken, in the way. That narrative shaped so much of how I operated in early leadership. I tried to prove I belonged. I overcompensated. I poured myself into work, because it was the one place I felt like I could earn love. Even in that confusion, God was planting something deeper. Teachability was born not in the classroom, but in the chaos. It taught me that leadership isn't about being first, it's about being faithful. Sometimes, the best leaders are the ones who've had to fight through the fear of being forgotten. That fear shaped me, but it didn't finish me. It prepared me to lead with empathy. To see the kid in the back of the room. To value the quiet staff member. To notice the one who's always giving but never asking. Because I know what it feels like to be in the room, but not feel like you matter. That, more than any title or training, has made me the kind of leader I want to be.

At 18, while attending the College of the Sequoias, I started working at a wonderful community organization. By nineteen, I was promoted to full-time. My first real boss, Dave, saw something in me. He entrusted me with responsibility including day camps, after-school programs, youth sports—and gave me the space to figure out who I was. I was terrified of sports. I wasn't an athlete. I quickly learned that leadership wasn't about being the expert; it was about building a team, empowering others, and serving people well. I organized volunteers, created systems, and elevated customer service. As a result, our programs thrived.

Something else extraordinary happened at that time, I met Laura. A woman whose love would forever change my life. We started as friends, and over time, she became my best friend, my confidant, and my partner in everything. My early years in Visalia gave me more than just a job. They gave me an identity. They gave me purpose. They gave me love.

I didn't know childcare, camps, teens, family programming or sports, but I was encouraged to learn and find ways to ensure people had the services they deserved. I didn't always know the right way to lead every program or even where to begin. I had never run a childcare center or led a teen leadership program. I didn't have a background in family engagement or recreation planning. When I was asked to oversee camps, I had no idea how to manage schedules, licensing, or the complexities of summer staffing. I knew how to ask. I reached out to people who had walked the path before me; veteran teachers, camp counselors, front desk staff, site directors, and parents who knew what their communities needed. I listened. I observed. I rolled up my sleeves and learned everything I could, not because I was expected to know it all, but because I believed the people we served deserved my best. In that process, I discovered one of the most important truths of leadership: you don't have to be an expert to lead, you just have to be humble enough to learn and wise enough to empower the people who are already experts in their own right.

> *"Everyone should be quick to **LISTEN**, slow to speak and slow to become angry."*
>
> – JAMES 1:19 (NIV)

Life kept shaping me as I moved from city to city, from role to role. Sometimes the shaping came through feedback I didn't want to hear. Sometimes it came through failure, disappointment, or grief. Sometimes it came through moments of unexpected grace, like when someone gave me a second chance, trusted me with more responsibility, or told me they saw something in me I couldn't yet see in myself. That's the gift of being teachable. You open yourself to the shaping, even when you're still shattered.

FROM SHATTERED TO SHAPED

Teachability is born in the gap between who you are and who you know you're called to be. It's forged in the moments when everything feels broken, but something in you still whispers, "Keep learning." That whisper has carried me through some of the most painful seasons of my life, not just because I wanted to survive, but because I believed I could still grow.

There's a misconception that growth only happens when things are stable. That's simply not true. Some of my most transformative learning came in seasons of instability. In fact, it was in the shattering that God often did His best shaping. When you've built your life around predictability, safety, and titles, it's easy to confuse comfort for maturity. True maturity, the kind that marks great leaders happens when you're willing to be reshaped, even when it hurts.

Failure has taught me more about love, humility, and growth than any success ever could. If I could go back, I wouldn't ask for a perfect past, I'd ask for an open heart sooner. Because failure only becomes wisdom when you stop defending yourself long enough to feel it.

If you want to measure someone's teachability, don't look at how they handle success look at how they handle failure. The truth is, success often hides our blind spots. It reinforces what we already believe about ourselves and can lull us into thinking we've figured things out. Failure, on the other hand, is the great revealer. It humbles. It confronts. It strips away the polish and asks, "Are you still willing to grow when it costs you something?"

I've failed at every stage of leadership. I've made bad hires, overpromised and underdelivered, spoken too quickly in meetings, and not listened closely enough to the people right in front of me. I've become so focused on strategy that I forgot about spirit. I've let ego, stress, and the pressure to perform cloud my judgment. There are entire chapters of my leadership journey I wish I could rewrite. Here's what I've learned: failure only becomes fatal when you refuse to learn from it.

Teachability shows up in how quickly you can pivot after something goes wrong. I've seen leaders spend so much time trying to spin or justify a mistake that they miss the opportunity to grow from it. When you admit it, own it, and ask, "What can I do differently next time?" that's where transformation happens. That posture doesn't just impact you. It gives your team permission to do the same. It creates a ripple effect of humility, honesty, and forward momentum.

Even personally, I've had seasons where failure felt overwhelming. I've made mistakes in parenting, in friendships, and in faith. There have been moments when I didn't listen to God's prompting, chose comfort over conviction, or let fear of perception silence my voice. Every one of those failures, when processed through the lens of teachability, became sacred ground. A place where God wasn't punishing me, but preparing me for the next chapter.

Failure doesn't mean you're done. It means you're becoming. It means the lesson you're learning now might be the wisdom someone else needs later. It means you have a choice: to either let failure define you or let it refine you. I promise you, if you let it refine you, it will be one of the greatest teachers of your life.

LIVING THE LESSON: WHAT IT TAKES TO BE TEACHABLE

Teachability isn't a phase. It's not a workshop you attend once or a checkbox on your leadership résumé. It's a posture; a way of seeing the world, of receiving truth, and of responding to challenges with courage instead of defensiveness. It's a trait that must become part of your daily rhythm if you want to lead with depth and authenticity.

In my life, teachability has often shown up in uncomfortable ways. Not when I was sitting in a classroom or reading a leadership book, but when someone challenged me in a way I didn't see coming. A board member who questioned a decision I was sure about. A staff member who pointed out something I'd said that unintentionally hurt them. A friend who loved me enough to tell me I was wrong. In those moments, the easy thing would've been to get defensive or to justify. I've learned that defensiveness is the enemy of growth. If your first response is to protect your pride, your potential will never fully develop.

Teachability is humility in action. It's the ability to say, "I don't know," and not feel shame in it. It's the decision to make space for voices other than your own. It's understanding that leadership isn't about always being right, it's about always being open. Some of the best decisions I've made in my career came from a voice I almost didn't listen to, because I thought I had the answer. But the moment I paused, leaned in, and invited their insight, something better was born.

It also means being willing to receive truth from people who aren't in positions of power. I've had teenagers teach me how to lead with authenticity. I've had janitors remind me what service looks like. I've had part-time staff offer insights that changed how I saw a problem. Every time I allowed myself to be taught by someone who didn't have a title, I became a better leader. You don't need someone's approval to learn from them. You just need the eyes to see and the ears to hear.

Here's the hard truth: teachability isn't glamorous. It's not a moment you post about on LinkedIn or a story that always gets applause. It's the silent, consistent work of opening your heart even when you're tired. It's asking for feedback after a meeting, you know, didn't go well. It's reading the tough email twice before responding. It's apologizing without an excuse. It's being faithful in the small corrections so you don't have to be humbled by the big ones.

I've seen leaders rise fast because of their talent and fall just as fast because of their pride. I've seen others, slower to start, quieter in their approach, grow into extraordinary influencers because they never stopped learning. They knew their value didn't come from pretending to be perfect, it came from being willing to grow. That's the kind of leader I want to be. If you're reading this, I believe it's the kind you want to be, too.

RECALCULATING: THE WILLINGNESS TO STAY CURIOUS

If you want to lead anything; your family, your team, your business, your classroom, your church, then teachability must become your foundation not your backup plan. Not your fallback when things go wrong. Your starting point. Because without teachability, your growth will eventually plateau, and your influence will quietly begin to shrink. People will stop bringing you feedback. You'll stop seeking wisdom. Eventually, you'll be left wondering why things aren't moving forward like they used to.

The truth is, teachability doesn't make you weak. It makes you trustworthy. When your team knows that you're willing to listen, to adapt, to grow, they'll lean in. They'll take risks. They'll bring their real selves to the table. Because teachability doesn't just build better leaders. It builds healthier cultures. It makes it safe for others to learn, too.

This trait isn't developed in a vacuum. It takes practice. Intentionality. Vulnerability. You develop it every time you stop talking and start listening. Every time you ask a deeper question, instead of defending a shallow answer. Every time you choose humility over ego and curiosity over control.

Maybe the most important thing to remember is this: teachability isn't just for your professional life. It's for your soul. It's the posture you bring to God. The openness you carry into your relationships. The softness that allows you to see people not as threats, but as teachers. Because everyone and I mean everyone has something to offer you if you're willing to see it.

You won't always get it right. I know I haven't. If you stay committed to learning, to listening, to leaning in even when it's hard, you will keep growing. When you grow, the people you lead grow too.

That's how leadership works. That's how legacy is built. That's why teachability matters.

The world rewards confidence, but leadership rewards humility. Teachability is humility in motion.

Teachability is not about insecurity. It's not playing small or pretending you don't know anything. It's the posture of someone who knows they haven't arrived yet and doesn't plan to. It's curiosity in a culture of certainty. The moment you stop learning, you start losing relevance.

The greatest downfall of talented leaders isn't failure, it's stagnation. They get promoted, get praise, and stop growing. They coast on what worked five years ago and forget the world changed around them. Their ego gets louder than their listening. I know this, because I have made this mistake, over and over again.

The most valuable leaders I know? They stay hungry to learn. They read. They ask questions. They take notes, even in meetings where they're the most experienced person. They say things like, "Tell me more," and, "I've never thought of it that way." They don't fear feedback, they chase it.

If you're teachable, you'll never be irrelevant. You may stumble. You may get passed over for flashier personalities. In the long game? You win. Because teachability compounds. It evolves. It multiplies. One day, you'll be the most prepared person in the room, not because you had all the answers, but because you never stopped asking better questions.

REFLECTION QUESTIONS

Take time to write, journal, or meditate on these before moving to the next chapter:

- What have been the greatest teachers in your life—people, pain, or pivotal moments? How did those experiences shape the way you lead today?
- Where in your leadership are you tempted to believe you "already know"? What would it look like to approach that area with humility and openness?
- Who in your team, family, or circle do you need to learn from, rather than lead? How can you make space for their voice?
- Are there wounds in your story that you've overlooked as lessons? What might God be trying to teach you through them?
- What does teachability look like in your relationship with God? Are you still listening, still learning, still following?

Nothing
moves

until a
leader
does.

chapter two

INITIATIVE
THE DRIVE TO MAKE IT HAPPEN

"Teachability opens the door. Initiative walks through it. Leadership is not about waiting for the perfect moment— it's about acting when no one else will."

START BEFORE YOU'RE READY

If teachability is the willingness to learn, initiative is the decision to act on what you've learned, especially when it's hard, unpopular, or unclear. If there's one thing I've learned over the years, it's this: nothing moves until a leader does.

There's a version of leadership the world celebrates, and then there's the version that actually creates change. The celebrated version is cautious, curated, and calculated. It waits for conditions to be perfect, for the path to be paved, and for every piece to be planned. The version that changes lives? It's bold. It's messy. It moves through chaos. It steps forward when the lights are still off. The most transformational leaders I've ever met weren't the most polished. They were the ones who acted when no one else would.

When I look back on my own journey, I can't count the number of times I've been dropped into situations that were unclear, broken, or stuck. Places where the easiest thing to do was to maintain the status quo. I've never felt called to maintenance. I've felt called to motion. There's something in my wiring that won't let me sit still when something can be better. It's that inner voice, that stirring, that has fueled my entire journey in leadership.

MOTION CREATES MOMENTUM

Poll Question: When facing uncertainty in leadership, which action do you find most difficult?

- Waiting for the "perfect" plan
- Moving forward with fear and uncertainty
- Taking responsibility before others step in
- Seeking help from others

I learned early in my career that I had to move forward, even when I was not entirely clear on the next step. As I said, motion creates its own momentum. I started to see the importance of drive when I was 24. I got a promotion without a clear path for how to do the job I found myself in. I was surrounded by people who were older, more experienced, and, in many ways, more prepared. I didn't let that stop me. I moved. I asked questions. I sought out mentors. I worked late. I watched how leaders carried themselves, and then I practiced when no one was looking. When opportunities came, opportunities most people would've waited years to take, I raised my hand. Not because I was ready, but because I was willing.

That's initiative. It's not about waiting until the fear goes away. It's about stepping in while your hands still shake. I remember the first time I had to sit down and have a real conversation with one of my kids about something they were struggling with; emotionally, mentally, spiritually. I didn't grow up with those kinds of talks. Vulnerability wasn't modeled for me. I didn't have a roadmap for how to lead with tenderness or how to guide someone through pain without trying to fix it. I knew it mattered. So I sat there, heart racing, unsure of the right words, but fully present. I didn't need a script, I needed courage. That moment, awkward as it was, changed our relationship. That's the kind of initiative leadership really demands; not flashy ideas, but the guts to show up for people when it's uncomfortable, when you're unqualified, when silence would be easier. Sometimes, that's where the most transformational leadership begins, not in your expertise, but in your effort to show up anyway.

Momentum is a funny thing. People wait for it to show up. It doesn't appear on its own. It's created by movement. Motion creates momentum. A well-timed conversation, a simple act of courage, an early decision no one sees, that's how cultures begin to shift. That's how teams start to believe again.

That's how stale organizations get oxygen again. The greatest momentum in my career hasn't come from strategy documents. It comes from decisions to move, one faithful step at a time.

WHEN INITIATIVE COSTS YOU

Let's be honest: initiative is not always applauded. In fact, sometimes it gets you into trouble. The cost of the initiative hasn't just been professional, it's been personal. I've had board members who once cheered me on suddenly turn cold when the direction changed or the truth got too uncomfortable. I've faced volunteers who crossed boundaries, trying to control, manipulate, or steer the mission for their own agenda. Staff I once trusted as friends used our closeness for convenience, not commitment. Even in my own family, I've been leaned on more for what I could give than for who I was. The initiative exposed all of that. When you move, people show their true colors. Some celebrate you. Others tolerate you. A few, well, they'd rather see you shrink than shine. That kind of betrayal stings. It tempts you to stop trying, to play it safe. I've learned this: the pain of being used doesn't outweigh the purpose of being called. Leadership will cost you comfort. If you let it, it will teach you what and who is worth carrying forward.

Here's the truth: for every board member who resisted, another rose up with vision. For every volunteer who tried to control, there were two more who caught the heart of the mission and gave selflessly. For every friendship that faded under pressure, others were forged in trust, accountability, and mutual respect. For every hard moment with family, I've also seen reconciliation, restoration, and growth. Initiative doesn't just reveal the people who can't go with you, it introduces you to the ones who were always meant to. Over time, you build something stronger. A team that shares your values. A culture that breathes with purpose. A mission that can bend without breaking. That's the reward of staying the course. Not perfection, but alignment. Not ease, but impact. Not applause, but peace. That kind of success? It's worth every scar.

Some people don't want to be moved. They find comfort in their routines and the predictability of systems that no longer serve the mission. When you show up with ideas, energy, and a spark, they might resist, especially if you're doing it with honesty. Especially if you're willing to call out what's no longer working.

I've lost friends because I moved too quickly. I've made enemies by rocking boats that others were desperate to keep steady. I've been accused of moving too fast, disrupting the norm, or pushing too hard. Sometimes, yes, I've gotten it wrong. I've also seen what happens when leaders wait too long. Missions shrink. Good people leave. Communities suffer. The risk of waiting often outweighs the risk of moving.

Initiative demands courage, but it also requires discernment. Not every move is wise, and not every fight is yours to pick. I'd rather lead with courage and correct it than lead with fear and regret it. The world is full of dreamers who waited too long. I don't want to be one of them.

Dreaming is not the only reason people hold back. I have lived my life believing that you can't be afraid to lose your job or you'll make bad decisions. People are so scared of displeasing people that they don't make change and they get stuck. Initiative is having the courage to call out the obvious. If you see a family in need, help them. If you see something that does not align with the mission of the organization, change it.

When I speak about initiative and what gets in the way, I've brought a full-sized rowboat on stage with me. I tell folks, in order to move forward, you're going to need to jump into the rowboat with me. Grab an oar, and we'll paddle forward towards where we need to go. Some of you will do it. Some of you will get in the boat and bring your doubt and will question everything that's happening. That's like holding the oar in the water without moving it, slowing us down. Some of you are going to jump in the boat and face the other direction and paddle the other way. This is why an organization will keep spinning in circles. If we believe we have to agree on everything to move forward, we are stuck. Sometimes initiative requires risk because you need to row without all the answers or full agreement. Sometimes it requires risk because I am going to need to kick people off the boat to move forward.

THE SACRED WEIGHT OF GOING FIRST

One of the most difficult parts of leadership is that you often have to go first. You say the hard thing first. You apologize first. You show up first. You break the silence first. Going first is lonely. It exposes you. It makes you vulnerable. It also opens the door for everyone else to step forward.

There's a sacred weight to going first. It says, "I believe in what's possible more than I fear what's probable." When I stepped into a new role in Texas, the organization had been gutted by a global crisis. People were hurting. Systems were outdated. The culture was reactive and protective. I knew that if we were going to recover, someone had to go first. Someone had to speak the hard truths, reimagine what was possible, and lead with conviction instead of consensus. So I moved. When I did, people began to move too.

Being the first to act doesn't mean you always get it right. It means you care enough to try. Sometimes, that's all people need to see.

FAITH IN ACTION

Initiative isn't just a leadership principle, it's a spiritual posture. Faith, without works, is dead. So is leadership. I've learned time and again that faith without movement doesn't heal anything. It doesn't restore broken systems or rebuild trust. It doesn't comfort the grieving or lift the overlooked. Faith in action is the rhythm of a leader's life. It means showing up with your "yes" before you have all the details. It means trusting that God will meet you in the middle, not just at the finish line.

There were seasons when I was scared to move, scared to take a new job, scared to risk a new relationship, scared to say the thing I knew I needed to say. Every time I chose obedience over comfort, I saw fruit I couldn't have imagined. Every time I waited too long, I saw opportunities slip away.

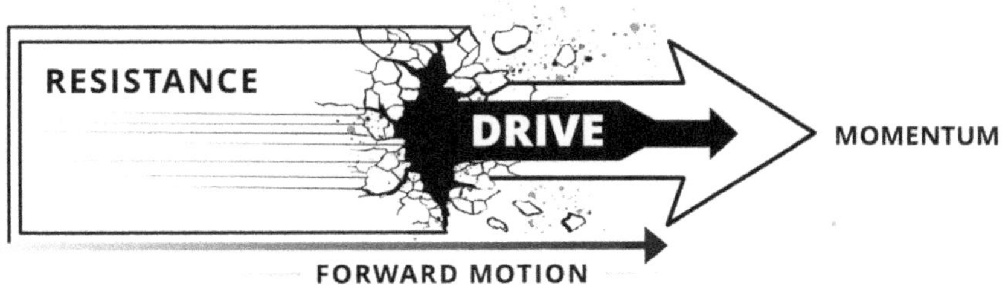

Drive turns resistance into momentum.

You won't always know what the outcome will be, but you can know your heart. You can know your reason. You can root your movement in purpose instead of pride. When you do, your steps start to matter more than your certainty.

WHEN NO ONE'S COMING—YOU STILL GO

One of the toughest truths a leader has to face is this: sometimes, no one's coming. No one's going to fix it for you. No one's going to knock on your door and hand you a roadmap. No one's going to give you the permission slip you're waiting for. It's you. You are the answer to the moment. You have to move, especially when you feel most unqualified.

I've had many of those moments in my life. Some were personal, like leading through grief or loving kids through their own trauma. Others were professional, walking into jobs that needed total reconstruction or teams that were fractured from poor leadership. In each case, the defining moment wasn't what I inherited. It was what I chose to do with it.

I've seen too many people wait for clarity that never comes. They overthink, overplan, and overpray, hoping the fear will disappear. The truth is, most fear is only defeated by motion. Action erodes anxiety. The longer we wait, the heavier our doubts grow. The second we start, even with small steps, things begin to change. Your mind shifts. Your body finds rhythm. Your courage rises. Waiting can be wise, but hesitation rooted in fear is a trap disguised as strategy.

The reality is, the call of leadership rarely comes with applause. It usually comes with weight, with silence, with a quiet whisper that says, "Go." If you've built your life on comfort, you'll miss it. If you've trained your spirit to recognize that nudge, to know when the time to move has come, you won't need a sign. You'll just move because you know it's who you are.

Initiative means you go even when the room is quiet. You speak up even when your voice shakes. You take the meeting that makes you uncomfortable. You have the conversation you've been avoiding. You take the risk that no one else is willing to take. Not because you're reckless, but because you know it's time.

YOU BUILD WHILE BLEEDING

Houston had become home. It was where I began to find myself professionally, where I walked the streets to bring programs to the community, where my voice started to matter, and where Laura and I built the foundation of our life together. I had a position that gave me purpose, a growing team that trusted me, and a wife who fully supported me. We were ready to take on the next chapter: parenthood.

The anticipation of becoming parents lit up every corner of our lives. We set up the nursery, and friends brought gifts. Our family was ready. It was our first child, and I had already imagined what it would be like to hold him, to watch him grow, to teach him to love others, and maybe even run cross-country like I once did. Life doesn't always follow the script you've written in your head.

When Laura was taken to the hospital, my heart raced with excitement. I remember crying with joy on the way there, thinking, this is the moment. This is the beginning of a new legacy. That ride didn't end the way I imagined. The words "complications" and "we're so sorry" blurred together into a fog of disbelief. Our son, Nathaniel Wyatt Brown, was born silent. No cries. No heartbeat. No future on this earth.

We held him in our arms for hours. We memorized every feature of his tiny face, every inch of his little body, and whispered promises into ears that would never hear us. As if the world wasn't already crashing down, we woke up the next morning to hear that the Twin Towers in New York had fallen. September 11, 2001. The entire country was grieving, and I was drowning in a personal 9/11 of my own.

In that hospital, I was approached by a group of Catholic nuns, kind-hearted and full of prayer. They didn't know that just days before, in my best friend's apartment, I had screamed, cried, and finally given my life to Christ. I had said yes to a God I had doubted for so long. Now here I was, holding my dead child, questioning everything.

I yelled. I cursed. I rejected their prayers. I felt punished. I felt betrayed. Deep inside, I carried the weight of a dangerous belief, that maybe God had it out for me. Maybe I was never meant to find peace. My faith didn't disappear that day, but it shattered into pieces that I wouldn't begin to pick up again for years.

> # "*Faith by itself, if it is not accompanied by* **ACTION**, *is dead.*"

> — JAMES 2:17 (NIV)

A NEW START AND A NEW CALLING

We needed to start over. Houston was full of memories, both beautiful and unbearable. So when a CEO role opened at a small, rural community organization in Georgia, I decided to take a leap. It was a long shot. I was young, grieving, and far from polished. Somehow, the board saw something in me, and I was offered the role.

We packed our lives and moved in with Laura's parents, ready to begin again. I was just 28 years old and suddenly in charge of an organization that didn't yet have a building. The smallest chartered chapter in the country. No blueprint. No staff. No roadmap. Just faith and vision. It was exactly the blank slate I needed; to rebuild, not just a community, but myself.

Georgia gave me room to grow as a leader and space to rediscover my voice. I learned how to fundraise, how to develop programs from scratch, and how to rally a community around a purpose. We built something from nothing. In the middle of that process, I received an invitation that would change me again: I was asked to be a youth pastor at our church.

Now I was leading both an organization and a youth ministry. It felt right. Like everything I had endured, it was finally pointing toward something deeper than just success. I was learning how to lead people's hearts, not just their habits. In that season of serving, our joy returned.

Laura became pregnant again, and this time, under close medical supervision, our daughter Abbie was born early, but healthy. I held her like she was the most fragile treasure in the world. This was our redemption moment. Our lion cub. Our miracle. Two years later, Colby joined our family. Life was full again. We had a home, a mission, and love that ran deep.

Even in that joy, leadership wasn't without pain. I would experience betrayal, hurt, and a level of spiritual rejection that tested me once again. My church, the very place that had welcomed me as a pastor and trusted me with their youth, decided, without warning, that I no longer fit. My initiative and my willingness to take risks and try new ways of being a church frightened the leadership. There was no conversation. No chance to explain. Just a statement: "We no longer sanction Mike Brown."

Just like that, I was out. No goodbye to the youth I had served. No closure for the families I had mentored. No time to discuss the growth that my initiative brought. No honoring that the families and the youth were well served by the changes we made. The hurt ran deep. It wasn't just a job lost, it was a family shattered. A spiritual community I had trusted. While I never stopped believing in God, I began to mistrust the people who claimed to represent Him.

I haven't returned to church in the same way since. I still believe. I still love Jesus. I've come to understand that church isn't just a building, it's a way of living. It's how you treat people. How you lead. How you show up when it's hard. My church became my home, my work, my circle. Through it all, God re-routed me again.

What no one tells you about initiative is how much of it happens while you're still hurting. You don't always get to move forward once everything is healed. Sometimes, the building begins while the wound is still fresh. That's real leadership. It's leading with a limp. It's making hard decisions with a heart still grieving. It's casting vision when your own world feels blurry.

Some of the most important leadership decisions I've made happened during the darkest seasons of my life: after loss, betrayal, and disappointment. I had every reason to pull back. To wait until I "felt better." But there's something holy about deciding to build anyway. It's one of the most profound forms of worship: choosing to keep going, not because it's easy, but because the people around you matter that much.

That's what initiative looks like. It's not leading from a stage, it's leading from a stretcher. It's not public victory, it's private obedience. Most people don't see it, but the ones who matter will feel it. They'll feel your presence. Your consistency. Your love. Your movement.

When the dust settles and the rebuilding starts to take shape, they won't remember how perfect your strategy was. They'll remember that you showed up, even when everything inside you wanted to disappear.

DISRUPTION IS NOT THE ENEMY—IT'S THE INVITATION

Initiative often comes disguised as disruption. It rarely looks like an open door with a welcome sign. More often, it looks like a wall falling down in front of you, followed by a whisper asking, "Now what?" Most people see disruption as a dead end. Leaders, true leaders, recognize it as an invitation to innovate.

I've been called a disruptor more than once in my career. Not because I wanted to stir the pot, but because I refused to settle. I couldn't walk into a room and pretend that dysfunction was okay. I wasn't interested in protecting the comfort of systems that weren't serving people. While that didn't always make me popular, it made me honest.

In leadership, you have to get comfortable being misunderstood. People who are committed to the status quo will always criticize those who dare to challenge it. When you step into a room with fresh ideas, real initiative, and a willingness to speak hard truths, don't expect everyone to clap. Expect some to leave. Expect pushback. Move anyway.

Initiative means stepping into disruption with purpose, not panic. It's about studying the cracks, asking the right questions, and building something stronger in the rubble of what didn't work. If you're leading well, people will eventually follow, not because you promised ease, but because you modeled courage.

Disruption can break you or build you. It depends on how you respond. If you see it as a punishment, you'll resist it. If you see it as God clearing space for something new, you'll embrace it. That shift in mindset is what separates good leaders from transformational ones.

WHAT YOU DO WHEN NO ONE IS WATCHING

Real initiative doesn't start in front of a crowd. It starts in the quiet moments, in the daily decisions no one sees. It's in the way you treat the front desk staff. In whether or not you return the shopping cart. In how you show up when you're tired, not just when you're celebrated.

There's a misconception that leadership begins with a title. Some of the most impactful leaders I've known didn't have one. They were camp counselors who showed up early and stayed late. They were front-line staff who noticed when a kid was sitting alone. They were volunteers who picked up trash without being asked. These people led through action, not applause.

Initiative is integrity in motion. It's doing the right thing when no one will thank you for it. It's staying late to help a teammate because you care, not because you're being evaluated. It's raising your hand to take responsibility when something goes wrong, even if you could easily blame someone else. That's the kind of initiative that builds culture. The kind that earns trust. The kind that makes people feel safe enough to take initiative, too.

Initiative is contagious. When people see you lead with conviction, they feel empowered to rise with you. They begin to believe they can make a difference too. That ripple effect? That's where legacy begins.

THE COURAGE TO KEEP SHOWING UP

Initiative doesn't guarantee results. It doesn't promise applause, validation, or instant breakthroughs. What it does promise is growth. Every time you show up, every time you move forward when quitting would be easier, you're planting something. Even if you don't see the fruit right away, faith tells you to keep planting.

There were moments in my life when showing up felt like the hardest thing in the world. Walking into staff meetings after burying my wife. Leading community forums when my own sons were spiraling. Putting on a smile at a ribbon-cutting while grieving silently inside. Initiative in those moments didn't feel brave, it felt like survival. I kept showing up. Every time I did, I found a little more strength than I had the day before.

What I've learned is that initiative isn't just about the first move, it's about the next one. And the one after that. It's about faithfulness over flash. It's about building even when the foundation feels cracked. It's about trusting that if you lead with love and honesty, the people who are meant to walk with you will find their way to your side.

You might not always get it right. I certainly haven't. I've said the wrong thing, hired the wrong people, acted out of frustration, and pushed too hard. The most important part of leadership isn't perfection, it's presence. It's being willing to try again. To apologize. To adjust. To keep moving forward, even when the last step didn't go as planned.

That's initiative. It's not flashy. It's faithful.

RECALCULATING: THE COURAGE TO MOVE FIRST

Initiative doesn't wait for applause. It doesn't ask for permission. It sees the need and moves toward it, before it's safe, perfect, or someone else gives you a green light.

Too many gifted people are sitting on the sidelines of their own calling, waiting for someone to invite them in. The truth is if you're always waiting for clarity, you'll never lead through chaos. Leadership is always born in chaos.

In every place I've led, initiative has made the difference between survival and transformation. The ones who make the biggest impact aren't always the ones with the most polished resumes. They're the ones who lean in. Who steps up? Who says, "What else can I do?" and then actually does it.

Initiative doesn't always look dramatic. Sometimes, it's sending that follow-up email. Sometimes, it's fixing the printer before anyone else notices it's broken. Sometimes, it's raising your hand and saying, "I don't know how, but I'll figure it out."

That's what real leaders do.

They act without being asked, take responsibility without being assigned, and step into the uncomfortable because they know movement creates momentum.

Maybe most importantly, initiative permits others to rise. Every time you go first, someone else realizes they can, too. Your courage becomes contagious. Soon, the culture started to shift, not because you told people what to do, but because you showed them what was possible.

I am a visionary and I have a lot of ideas. Sometimes people get burned out on the ideas but sometimes it lights a fire and people find they are passionate and can move mountains to make it happen. There was an idea I had about creating a recording studio for kids to give them access to music and recording. At our organization, everything's always about sports and fitness. What do you do with kids that aren't into that?

One of my staff took initiative and gathered people together, blocked off a portion of the building, and constructed an entire state of the art recording studio with grant funds. I wasn't allowed to go see it. They wanted to surprise me. They even recorded a group of kids, invited the community, and held an event where I got to experience the studio at the same time as the community. To me that was like, "Wow, you guys made something happen on your own. You were passionate about it. You took the initiative, and you just rolled with it. You found the funds, you found the way, you found the people. You've gathered people, and you made something happen. Best of all, it didn't take me outlining everything to do it."

That sounds extraordinary but it happens every time your kids take initiative and decide, hey, my parents were on vacation, and I guess maybe we should mow the lawn and clean the house, right? So when they get home, they don't have all this work to do. Initiative is born out of caring for people and being passionate about giving them what they need.

REFLECTION QUESTIONS

- When have you been tempted to wait for "perfect timing"? What held you back and what would've changed if you had taken initiative sooner?
- Think of a time when you moved forward before you felt ready. What did you learn from that experience about your own resilience and growth?
- Who in your life right now is waiting on you to move, not just in position, but in presence, effort, or love?
- Are there areas in your leadership or personal life where fear is masking itself as "strategy"? How can you discern the difference?
- What would change in your team, your family, or your faith if you showed up with initiative even when no one asked you to?

You lead through the grind,

not just the glory.

chapter three

DISCIPLINE
WORKING TO GET RESULTS

"Success is the sum of small efforts,
repeated day in and day out." – Robert Collier

THE RUNNER'S ROAD

Inspiration starts the race. Discipline finishes it. I never set out to be impressive. I set out to survive, to show up and be a little better today than I was yesterday. I wasn't chasing greatness. I was chasing growth. Growth, I learned, doesn't happen in sprints. It happens in long-distance runs through seasons of silence, resistance, and fatigue. That's what discipline looks like: the quiet decision to keep going when the applause has stopped, when the emotion is gone, and when no one is watching.

Cross-country taught me that lesson early. I wasn't the fastest. I didn't win trophies. I ran every day. I trained, even when no one else showed up for practice. That sport didn't reward flash, it rewarded faithfulness. You'd run for miles with no finish line in sight, just the beat of your own heart and the pressure of your own willpower. That's what leadership often feels like. No grandstands. No medals. Just you, your mission, and your ability to keep moving.

It wasn't until I realized that my small efforts, shaving seconds off my time, impacted the whole team that I really understood what discipline means in leadership. Your discipline doesn't just affect you. It affects the people you're called to serve, love, and lead. Whether it's showing up to practice, preparing a message, or holding a hard boundary, every act of discipline builds a better future for everyone in your life.

Research from the Journal of Applied Sports Psychology shows that athletes who develop discipline in training, especially in long-distance running, have better mental endurance and higher success rates in both sports and life challenges. Discipline doesn't just improve physical performance, but mental resilience as well.

THE MICROPHONE

I didn't step into leadership with confidence. I stepped in with questions, insecurities, and the faint hope that maybe, just maybe, I could make a difference.

My first job didn't come with a title or a paycheck worth writing home about. It came with a microphone and a camp full of kids who needed a reason to sing. I hesitated, unsure and inexperienced. But I said yes. That's where it all began.

Boom-chicka-boom.

That silly camp song changed everything. For the first time, I heard my voice echoed back in laughter, energy, and joy. More than that, I realized something crucial: leadership doesn't always begin in a boardroom. It begins where people need you most. Those kids didn't need a perfect leader. They needed presence. Energy. Consistency. Someone who cared enough to show up and make things just a little better.

I did. Every day. Even on days when I didn't feel like it.

Discipline is what carried me through that first summer and every season since. It's what turned a moment of fun into a lifelong calling. It's what shaped my voice, not just for camp songs, but for vision casting, conflict resolution, and leadership in high-stakes moments. It's what prepared me for ministry, for fatherhood, for grief, and for growth.

Passion may hand you a microphone. Discipline teaches you how to use it.

THE REAL WORK BEHIND REAL MINISTRIES

Years later, I watched that lesson repeat itself in ministry.

The Youth ministry I talked about in the last chapter was not just about initiative and disruption, though those were important, but they needed to be followed up with discipline. We did a lot of good and brought a lot of kids into a relationship with the church. When I began leading youth, it didn't take long to realize the traditional models weren't landing, that is part of the disruption. The kids weren't moved by games or polished sermons, they were moved by presence. They didn't want a youth group. They wanted a place where they belonged.

So we built one. That was the initiative.

Real Ministries was born out of that hunger. A student-led band. A garage-turned-sanctuary. Worship nights filled with praise that wasn't polished, but real. Testimonies that sounded more like raw confessions than scripted speeches. Here's what most people missed: that kind of authenticity doesn't happen by accident. It takes discipline.

We didn't just show up on Sunday and wing it. We practiced. We rehearsed. We prayed. We wrote songs. We failed. Then we tried again. Discipline.

I'd show up at 9 p.m. after work shifts, music in hand, drained from a full day of leading, but I still poured into those teens. Because something sacred was forming in that mess. They weren't just learning chords and lyrics, they were learning calling. They were learning what it means to commit to something bigger than emotion. Over the course of this work young high school students had confidence and one in particular took over the leadership of the group, and others followed. To be honest, I should have walked off the stage and mentored from the back, but something said to me, even as uncomfortable as I was, that if I do this, they will too.

Discipline is what kept the lights on. It's what turned chaos into choreography. It's what raised up young leaders who still reach out to me today and say, "Thank you for showing up." I know I succeeded, even though the ending was painful, because those kids are now adults who keep in touch and let me know they were shaped by the discipline of mentoring through action and presence.

THE DISCIPLINE OF PRESENCE

Leadership isn't about power. It's about presence. Presence doesn't happen by accident, it's a discipline.

It's the daily decision to be there, to look someone in the eye when you're tired, to stay engaged when your heart is somewhere else. It's choosing to show up with full attention, even when your soul feels half-empty.

Real Ministries led to me leaving the church, and my heart broke over the loss and the confusion of doing the right thing for the youth and yet being pushed out for rocking the boat.

THE INVISIBLE WEIGHT OF LEADERSHIP

What most people don't see about leadership is how much of it happens in the dark, behind closed doors, off stage, and far from any applause. Discipline keeps you going when the weight of others' expectations feels heavier than your own hope.

I am jumping around in my life story here so that you can experience the importance of discipline. Building discipline gives us the foundation to lead, even in difficult or extraordinary circumstances. Even with tears in our eyes.

My wife Laura got sick, and everything changed. One day, we were planning for the future: vacations, kids' graduations, maybe a slower season.

THE DISCIPLINE PATH

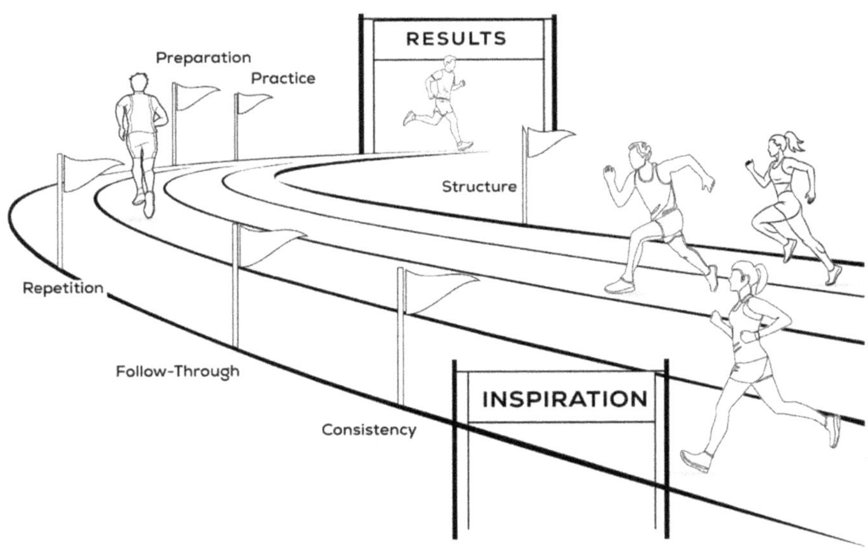

Discipline is what carries you when motivation fades;
it turns potential into progress.

Then a diagnosis stole all of it. Glioblastoma. Brain cancer. One of the worst kinds. One of the fastest.

Suddenly, presence wasn't a leadership principle. It was survival.

LEADING WHILE LOSING EVERYTHING

When I accepted the role in upstate New York, I saw it as another fresh start, a new challenge, a new team, a new community. I brought along my trusted chief of staff, someone who had walked through both the highs and lows with me before. We packed up our home, said another round of goodbyes, and headed north, filled with a sense of calling and optimism.

This chapter would test everything I thought I knew about leadership and about life.

At first, the job was everything I hoped it would be. There was potential, a mission to restore, and a team to build. My kids were in high school now, and while they were adjusting to a very different environment, we pressed forward. It was preppy. It was privileged. It was... unfamiliar. We pushed through, hoping that we had made the right choice.

Then came the diagnosis.

Laura, my wife, my partner, my best friend was diagnosed with glioblastoma. Brain cancer. The words alone shattered every plan, every routine, every sense of stability we had.

We were stunned. Then we were furious. At least, I was. I remember screaming at God, "Why her? Why now? Why this?" She was the sweetest person I'd ever known, a servant to others. A gentle soul. A mother who gave everything. This is what she got?

I begged God to take me instead. Told Him He had made a mistake. No miracle came.

What followed were the hardest months of my life. Doctor visits. Treatments. Watching the woman I loved fade before my eyes, losing her words, her smile, her strength and still trying to be a father. Still trying to lead an organization. Still trying to function as if life hadn't just shattered me.

Some staff showed up. My chief of staff, especially, carried a weight no one could have expected. He helped hold up the organization while I tried to hold up my family. Not everyone understood. Some saw it as an opportunity. Others judged from a distance. The volunteers who were supposed to support me? Many were silent.

We were alone, but Laura wasn't. Her family surrounded her, came often, sat by her bedside, helped in the home. Her parents were just a short drive away, and that gave me peace. I knew, deep down, God had rerouted us here for her. She needed that family. That presence. That goodbye.

The day she took her last breath, we were all there; her parents, her family, our kids, and me. The room was heavy and holy all at once.

And the next morning? In the middle of COVID, when the world had shut down, we heard it, hundreds of cars honking outside, slowly parading past our home. It was the funeral that wasn't allowed inside, but our community brought it to our front lawn. Love showed up. Just when I thought it was gone.

That parade didn't bring her back. It reminded me: we weren't forgotten. She wasn't forgotten. Neither was I.

There were moments I sat by her bedside while trying to return calls from donors. I'd write strategy decks while listening to her breathe through seizures. I'd sit on Zoom calls with a smile while her body quietly failed just feet away. I was leading people through organizational change while my life was unraveling in real time.

I never stopped showing up.

Not because I'm a hero. Because I knew what was at stake. My kids were watching. My team was watching. Most importantly, Laura was watching.

There were nights I collapsed in the hallway outside her room, completely broken. Days I drove in circles before going home, just to buy myself a few minutes to scream in the car. There were moments when I held her hand and begged God for a miracle, and when none came, I still had to pack lunches, attend staff meetings, and finish annual reports.

This is the truth of discipline: it doesn't make you a robot. It makes you faithful.

I held Laura as she slipped away. I watched her take her final breath surrounded by family, love, and music. The next morning, the grief crashed over me like a tidal wave. Yet, even then, God gave me the strength to hold our family together, to plan a celebration of life, travel to family, to honor her story, and to keep leading.

Not long after, I walked into work.

Not because I had healed. Because I had learned that healing and leading often walk hand in hand.

If you've ever loved someone who's dying, you know what presence really means. It means sitting still when you want to run. It means wiping someone's mouth or changing a bedsheet and doing it like it's sacred, because it is. It means holding your grief in one hand and your role in the other, and refusing to let go of either.

It didn't stop in grief either. It was only a few months after her passing that the challenge at work presented itself. Accusations of not being present, drinking obsessively, not holding down the job. I was told there were concerns. Not concerns for me or my family, but concerns for the organization. I had the courage and walked away, took time for myself, and began the much-needed reset that I needed to take back who I was. With this I kept quiet, I supported those during the transition. I didn't walk away from people, I loved them, I didn't become angry, I was hurt. I stayed present in the world.

That's the discipline of presence. Not just showing up, but staying present in the pain, the heartbreak, the complexity. Especially when it would be easier to check out.

Because the world doesn't need stronger leaders, it needs more present ones.

PAUSE & REFLECT

When have you been called to lead through heartbreak or loss?

- What did presence look like for you in that season?
- Who was watching you, and how did your decision to stay present impact them?
- Write down one way you can practice the discipline of presence today—in your work, in your family, or within yourself.

PARENTING, PARTNERSHIPS, AND PEOPLE YOU CAN'T FIX

Discipline is often framed as a solo act; waking up early, writing goals, sticking to a plan. Some of the hardest discipline I've ever practiced didn't involve waking up early. It involved staying up late, sitting with a child who

"*Let us not become weary in doing* **GOOD**, *for at the proper time we will reap a harvest if we do not give up.*"

– GALATIANS 6:9 (NIV)

wouldn't talk, listening to someone repeat the same mistake for the third time, and choosing not to give up on someone just because they've given up on themselves.

Discipline is loving people when it's hard.

Laura and I adopted two of our children as teenagers. I will tell their story in the next chapter. When we adopted our sons as teenagers, I quickly realized that love alone wouldn't be enough. Love starts the story, but discipline is what carries it through the messy chapters. Our sons were angry, rightfully so. They had been through things no child should have to endure. We soon understood that this wouldn't be a clean, redemptive story. It would be a war.

I've sat through slamming doors, shattered dishes, and whispered prayers through tears. I've had to repeat the same values over and over again. I've had to set boundaries that broke my heart but built their future. Now, years later, they are rebuilding their lives; slowly, imperfectly, beautifully. As those boys got older, I had to create a boundary and stop enabling them. So I stopped. No more money, no more visits, and the words, this might be the last time I see you alive, but I have come to peace with that. A discipline that was the hardest parental decision I have ever made.

That is the fruit of discipline.

Discipline doesn't only show up at home. It also manifests in how we treat our teams, colleagues, spouses, and friends. It's the discipline of grace reminding ourselves that people are not problems to solve, but souls to shepherd.

There's discipline in not reacting immediately. In pausing. In praying before responding. There's discipline in not firing someone on the spot, even if your gut tells you to. There's discipline in continuing to believe in someone, even when others have written them off.

Because people don't always grow when it's convenient. Leadership isn't just about building systems, it's about building people.

I build people up to help them make decisions about priorities to avoid burnout. There are a lot of conflicting projects going on at any one time and if we pay attention to them all we will crash and burn. I use the example of a jar of rocks to help people see that they are letting themselves get overwhelmed. I take a jar, a large, clear container, and first, I put in some large rocks. These are the priorities—the most important things we need to get done and when they are all that's in the container, they're easy to see. Then I put in smaller rocks—all the little ideas we see and think we should act on also. These bury the big rocks, the priorities, and get in the way, but we can still see our priorities. Next, I pour in sand. This is the fluff which drowns out everything else. Then, I fill the container up with water and shake it. That's the chaos of life that keeps all the contents swirling around when we are trying to get anything done.

When we try to reach for one of the priorities, we can't find it so we do what we can grasp. Reaching for every little thing fills up our time but does not get the actual job done. People can be working hard, all the time, but on all the wrong things. It takes discipline to find the priorities and not allow anything to get in the way of getting them done. Discipline helps us to get to our passions and not let them get lost in the craziness.

Discipline without passion is just boring. We can work on the checklist items, and the tiny things and lose our connection to our passion. Discipline helps us get back to it. It keeps us focused on the right things every day. Passion reminds us why we started, and discipline helps us finish.

REAL WORLD DISCIPLINE

You don't have to look far to see the cost and reward of discipline in others.

All of these are examples of real world discipline in action:

- A mother working multiple jobs to support her family
- A teacher working to inspire unmotivated students
- Someone in recovery, staying clean one day at a time
- A civil rights leader who took a stand despite adversity

Think of a mother who works three jobs to keep her children fed. She doesn't wake up every morning with excitement. She wakes up because she has a calling.

Think of a teacher who shows up every day to a classroom where some kids don't want to be taught. She prepares lesson plans, stays late to grade, and still writes encouraging notes to students who push her buttons.

Think of someone in recovery, attending meetings, working the steps, staying clean one day at a time. That's discipline. That's courage in motion.

Think of the civil rights leaders who marched when no one would stand beside them. Who chose nonviolence when violence knocked at their door? That's discipline too.

Discipline isn't reserved for CEOs or pastors. It belongs to every single person who chooses to keep showing up when the easy thing would be to quit.

THE RHYTHMS THAT SAVE YOU

One of the greatest myths about discipline is that it's about pushing through: working harder, doing more. Real discipline understands the value of rest, of retreat, of rhythm.

After Laura died, I wanted to disappear. Not for a day, but for good. I didn't think I could lead again, love again, or even breathe right. I learned that discipline is what saves you when everything else breaks.

I built new habits. Not massive ones, simple ones.

- Morning walks with my kids
- Quiet time in Scripture, even if I was angry at God
- Calling my friends back instead of isolating
- Scheduling time to laugh, to cry, to be human

Leaders aren't machines. We are emotional, spiritual, relational beings. If we want to lead for the long haul, we have to practice the discipline of being human, of sabbath, of saying "no," of accepting help.

Discipline doesn't always look like doing more. Sometimes, it looks like finally doing less on purpose.

LEADERSHIP LESSON: DISCIPLINE – WORKING TO GET RESULTS

Discipline is not about punishment, it's about preparation. It's the scaffolding that holds up everything we hope to build. Passion may inspire you. Purpose may guide you. Discipline is what gets you across the finish line.

It's not glamorous. It's often thankless. Discipline is what keeps your name trustworthy, your leadership grounded, and your mission alive.

Discipline is in the decisions no one sees:

- Saying yes to the hard conversations.
- Saying no to shortcuts.
- Honoring your word when it costs you.
- Waking up early to prepare.
- Staying late to reflect.
- Creating boundaries so you don't burn out.
- Loving your people even when they're hard to love.

It is what makes ordinary leaders extraordinary.

The disciplined leader doesn't chase applause. They chase alignment. They don't need attention, they need traction. And they understand that legacy isn't built in loud moments, but in consistent ones.

Whether you're a CEO, a parent, a teacher, a coach, or simply someone trying to live with purpose, discipline is the engine that will get you where God has called you to go.

You don't have to be perfect. Just consistent. You don't have to have it all figured out. Just refuse to give up. You don't have to do it alone. God honors the steady heart.

Let the world chase results. You? Chase the rhythm that builds results that last.

RECALCULATING: THE BRIDGE BETWEEN DESIRE AND DESTINY

Discipline is not sexy. It doesn't trend on social media. It's not the exciting part of leadership, but it is the **essential** part.

Everyone wants the reward. Few want the repetition.

Discipline is showing up when it's boring, when no one's clapping. When the results are slow and your motivation is lower than your Wi-Fi signal. Leaders are made in those moments; those 6 AM alarms, those quiet decisions, those seemingly invisible habits.

I've seen what happens when leaders lack discipline. They burn bright and fade fast. They crush a keynote and crumble in follow-through. They have bursts of genius, but no rhythm to carry them.

The disciplined leader? They're steady. They're trusted. They build reputations on reliability, not just charisma.

That's the kind of leader the world needs. Not perfect, Predictable. Not always flashy, Faithful.

Because you can't inspire people with inconsistency, and if your team doesn't know which version of you will show up today, they'll stop showing up with their best.

Discipline builds trust, and trust is the real currency of leadership.

Discipline is what makes your leadership matter. Not your talent. Not your timing. Not your resume.

Discipline is the choice to wake up and move forward when you don't feel like it. The faith to believe that doing the right thing over and over again will bear fruit, even if it takes time. The willingness to become the kind of leader people can count on.

You don't have to be the smartest. Or the most charismatic. Or the most experienced. Just be the one who keeps showing up. Because, in the end, that's what shapes the future.

REFLECTION QUESTIONS

Take time to pause, write, or talk through these questions. Leadership is formed in reflection just as much as in action.

- Where in your life have you seen the fruit of quiet discipline? What did that experience teach you about showing up?
- What rhythms or habits in your current season feel rushed, inconsistent, or unsustainable? What needs to change?
- Think about your home. Your relationships. Are you showing up there with the same level of consistency as you do in your work?
- What does rest look like for you? Are you practicing the discipline of restoration or are you running on empty?
- Who in your life has modeled powerful discipline? What can you learn from their example and how can you express your gratitude to them?

*This work
isn't just work.*

*It's people.
It's purpose.
It's legacy.*

chapter four

PASSION
RELATIONAL AND MISSION-FOCUSED

"Passion is not just about grand dreams and loud moments; it often begins in the silence of survival." – Anonymous

THE FIRE YOU DIDN'T ASK FOR

Studies have shown that childhood adversity, such as growing up in a single-parent household or experiencing trauma, can significantly influence the development of resilience and passion later in life. Resilience is often born in the face of hardship and struggle, shaping the individual into someone who not only survives but thrives.

In overcoming adversity, we discard what is not essential and we see what sustains us. These passions give us direction and purpose. We develop the strength to follow our passions and ambitions through purpose and meaning. This adversity forms us into who we are and gives us the strength to live it out in our lives.

I didn't know it back then, but passion started forming in me before I had words for it. It didn't come from a podium, a church, or a campfire moment, it came from chaos. From watching a single mom carry the weight of the world while still trying to hold her kids together. From being a quiet kid who stayed in the background, unnoticed, picked on for what I wore or how I looked. Passion didn't start as confidence. It started as survival.

My mom was young when she had me. Divorced before I turned five, she didn't have a blueprint for raising three kids in a world that never made it easy. She worked. She fought. She carried pain from abusive relationships and heartbreaks that no child should have to witness. But she stayed. Even though I didn't see it clearly back then, I see it now, her passion wasn't loud, but it was real. She had every reason to give up, but she didn't. She kept showing up, broken and tired, because that's what passion does.

As a kid, I didn't understand. I needed her to see me, to know my pain, to protect me from things she didn't even know I was carrying. I had my own trauma, my own silence, and it was growing louder inside me every day. She leaned on me to help with my brother and sister, not knowing I was unraveling inside. Our relationship became strained. I pulled away. After my suicide attempt, I had to leave. I needed to find myself. For years, our connection was scattered; sometimes close, sometimes cold. I blamed her for the pain I hadn't learned how to name yet.

Passion works backward sometimes. As I've grown older, I've come to see that her survival was love. Her grind was her way of saying, "I care." She didn't have the language, but she had the drive. That realization changed how I see her. It changed how I see myself.

THE LOVE THAT DIDN'T SAY "I LOVE YOU"

My dad was different. He didn't carry the same emotional weight in his voice, but he carried presence. He loved horses. He loved the land. He loved working with his hands. He wasn't the kind of man who said, "I love you," but he showed it; in quiet drives, in working side-by-side, in always being there when I needed him. He didn't speak much, but he was always around. Passion doesn't always shout. Sometimes, it just stays.

When I moved in with my dad and stepmom, something in me began to settle. They gave me a different kind of rhythm, a slower kind of love. My grandparents, God bless them, called me "Peanut" from the day I was born. They were proud of me before I even knew what there was to be proud of. That nickname followed me into every room, whispering a quiet truth: someone saw something in me long before I ever proved anything.

What kind of legacy plants seeds? Seeds that don't bloom until decades later, but when they do, they grow deep.

RE-ROUTED, RESTORED, REBUILT

Deep within me, I heard a whisper: "This is it. This is the place where everything you've been through will finally make sense." The losses. The failures. The cross-country moves. The pain. The growth.

In Fort Worth, I discovered a new purpose. A new team. A new chapter. I also encountered an older version of myself, the one who still believed that leadership could change lives.

When I stepped into a new organization it wasn't a celebration, it was a crisis. COVID had torn through our systems, strained our finances, and fractured our teams. Morale was low, and there were days I seriously questioned whether I had taken on more than I could carry. Discipline told me to show up again tomorrow. Rebuilding wasn't glamorous. It meant hard decisions, countless one-on-one conversations, and sleepless nights crafting vision decks and capital strategies; all while managing grief, team turnover, and deep fatigue. There were failures, but there was also faith. Through it all, I was reminded that leadership isn't about how loud you can speak but how consistently you can show up.

Back in Georgia, my early years as a leader, I helped organize foster care events and adoption programs, working alongside social workers to give children hope and homes. One of those workers once asked me, "Have you ever considered adopting?" And without hesitation, I said yes.

We always thought we'd adopt eventually. We imagined a younger child, someone who fit the age gap between Abbie and Colby. We didn't expect to be called into something bigger. Something bolder. Something that would challenge every belief we had about parenting.

Then we were introduced to two teenage brothers living apart in the foster system. We were asked to visit a boys' ranch under the guise of making a donation, with the boys giving us a tour.

I couldn't lie, not to them. When I introduced myself, I looked them in the eyes and said, "You know why we're really here. Let's not play games. Let's just get to know each other."

From that moment, something clicked. There was honesty. There was laughter. There was this sacred sense of belonging that none of us could explain. By the time we drove away that day, Laura and I knew. These boys were ours.

The process wasn't easy, as adoption rarely is. Our family grew, and our hearts expanded too. We now had four children; two biological, two adopted, and a new definition of family that didn't rely on blood, but on choice. Love became the glue. Grace became the rhythm. And chaos? Well, that became our new normal.

Not everyone understood our decision. Some questioned how we could bring teens into a house with younger children. Others whispered fears about trauma, rebellion, or safety. Here's what I learned: you don't adopt to rescue someone. You adopt because love demands a bigger table. Our table was always meant to have more seats.

Of course, it wasn't easy. There were angry nights. Emotional breakdowns. Fights, fears, and a steep learning curve on what trauma really looks like in a child. There were moments of joy and connection, and there were days we barely held it together. They were ours. Despite the chaos, despite the pain, love held us.

Life became my proving ground for love and kindness, the same kindness I had longed to receive but rarely did. It was time to lead differently. To lead with heart. To build a culture that healed, not just performed. To lead an organization not based on metrics, but on meaning.

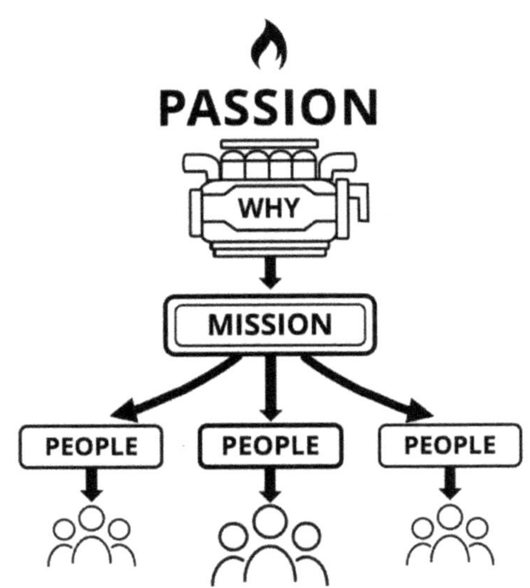

Passion without people is performance.
Passion connected to Mission becomes Legacy.

PASSION NEEDS A PLACE TO LIVE

Each piece below represents something you're passionate about. Your challenge is to identify which three pieces form the foundation of a healthy, sustainable passion and which ones may be warning signs of burnout.

Puzzle Pieces:
1. Serving others
2. Always saying "yes"
3. Taking time to rest
4. Ignoring your own needs
5. Staying connected to your "why"
6. Being available 24/7
7. Making space for family
8. Measuring success by busyness

REFLECTION QUESTION:

What three pieces will you choose to build a version of passion that is purposeful, grounded, and life-giving?

THE PART THEY DON'T TELL YOU

All of that, the chaos, the silence, the pride, the presence, it created this fire in me that said, "I'm going to build something different." I didn't want to see kids get ignored. I didn't want anyone to feel invisible like I did. I didn't want to repeat patterns of hurt and confusion. I wanted to make space. For people. For healing. For hope.

That's what led me to community organizations. That's what pulled me toward ministry. That's what still gets me out of bed every day. Passion isn't a job title or a motivational speech. It's a commitment to create what you never had. To fight for others the way you wish someone had fought for you.

Here's the part they don't tell you: passion will stretch you until you break. It will drive you to pour out until you're empty. It will convince you that you're doing God's work while quietly pulling you away from your family, your health, and your own soul.

I've missed birthdays. I've worked through anniversaries. I've carried other people's burdens so intensely that I forgot my own. Because when you're passionate, you often think you can't stop. You feel responsible for everyone's breakthrough. If you're not careful, you'll become the savior in your own story, when you were never meant to be.

I've had to learn that passion must be grounded. It must be balanced. You can love your calling without letting it consume you. You can serve people without sacrificing your family. You can pursue purpose without forgetting your own humanity.

THE HARDEST KIND OF PASSION

Sometimes, passion isn't exciting, it's exhausting. It's making the hospital visit when your tank is on empty. It's holding your dying wife's hand and then logging into a Zoom board meeting with a forced smile. It's showing up for a staff member who just betrayed you, because you still believe in them. It's refusing the easy way out when everything in you says, "You've done enough."

Passion is what made me fight for my sons when they didn't want me. It's what kept me praying when I had no words left. It fuels every message I write, every team I build, and every room I step into. It's also what nearly broke me.

I had to learn, often the hard way, that passion isn't about being the center of your own world. It's about making space in your world for others. You can only do that if you're healthy. You can only do that if your passion is fueled by love, not ego, by calling, not control.

WHEN PASSION CROWDS THE TABLE

Here's something I've only realized in hindsight: passion doesn't always ask permission. It barges in. It takes the front seat. It demands your time, your energy, your full attention and if you're not careful, it pushes everything else to the edges of the table.

That's exactly what happened in my life. I was so passionate about helping others that I forgot to help myself. I was passionate about building community, saving teenagers, developing leaders, launching programs, planting vision. Somewhere in the middle of it all, my friendships started to suffer. My marriage was tested. My relationship with my sister, brother, and parents. My connection to God began to feel more like a checklist than a relationship. Even my kids, the ones I would've laid down my life for, were getting what was left of me, not the best of me. I was pouring out everywhere but home.

It didn't happen overnight. It was gradual. One extra meeting. One more project. One late night turning into two. I kept telling myself it was just for a season. That it was all for a greater purpose. Passion without boundaries doesn't build, it burns. Before I knew it, the people I loved most were paying the price for the mission I was chasing.

There were birthdays I missed because I was trying to solve a crisis at work. Dinners where I was physically present but emotionally absent. Quiet drives home where I'd ask myself, "When was the last time you really laughed with your kids?" And I didn't like the answer.

That's the danger of unchecked passion, it convinces you that more is always better. Love isn't measured by how much you do. It's measured by how fully you show up. Presence requires restraint.

WHEN GOD BECAME BACKGROUND NOISE

Even my relationship with God, the source of everything I believe, was put on the back burner more times than I'd like to admit. I'd pray in transition. Worship during set-up. Read Scripture in a rush. I wasn't slowing down to be with Him. I was performing for Him. Passion for ministry started to overshadow my intimacy with the One who called me to it.

It's a sneaky thing, how spiritual passion can feel like obedience even when it's running on fumes. I had to come face-to-face with the reality that doing great things for God isn't the same as being with God. One is mission. The other is relationship. Passion must be rooted in relationship, or it turns toxic.

There were times I was on a stage preaching while feeling empty inside. Times when I was encouraging a staff team to hold onto their faith while privately wondering if mine was still intact. God, in His mercy, didn't let me spiral. He pulled me back, not with lightning bolts or breakdowns, but with gentle reminders.

In the silence after Laura passed. In the steady love of my children. In the grace of a new marriage I didn't think I deserved. In the people who showed up for me when I wasn't strong enough to lead them.

"Whatever you do, work at it with all your **HEART***, as working for the Lord."*

– COLOSSIANS 3:23

God was still there, still speaking, still calling, still inviting me to sit at His table, not as a leader, but as a son.

PASSION RECLAIMED

Now, I live differently. I lead differently. I've learned that real passion has rhythm. That loving people well means learning to love your own soul, too. I still work hard, I always will. I also rest. I protect time with my wife. I look my kids in the eyes. I go on walks. I sing again. I write for myself, not just for the crowd. I make space for God that isn't rushed or rehearsed.

Passion, when it's healthy, doesn't isolate, it integrates. It flows from identity, not insecurity. It creates space for others to be seen, because you're no longer trying to prove something.

That's what I want for every leader I help raise, not just a mission that drives them, but a heart that sustains them.

HELPING OTHERS FIND THEIR FIRE

There's a moment in every leader's life when passion shifts from something you carry to something you pass on. When I was younger, I thought passion had to be loud. I believed you had to grab the mic, cast the vision, rally the team, and carry the energy on your back. Real leadership isn't about being the loudest in the room, it's about lighting a flame in others that keeps burning long after you're gone.

These days, I spend more time building leaders than building programs. I look for the spark, the quiet hunger in someone's voice when they talk about the mission, the way they lean in during tough conversations, the way they stay late not for recognition, but because they care. That's passion. My role is to protect it, nurture it, and make sure it doesn't burn them alive.

I've mentored leaders who came in full of fire, only to nearly lose it, because no one taught them how to carry it. No one warned them how heavy leadership can be. No one showed them how to rest. No one gave them permission to say no to good things so they could say yes to the right things. I've watched people break under the weight of their own desire to make a difference.

So now I teach them what I wish someone had taught me: passion must be stewarded. It must be sustained with rest, truth, trusted community, and time with God. Otherwise, it turns into performance. Performance is a trap, because the applause always fades. When it does, you'll either find yourself… or lose yourself.

THE PASSION TO LEAD… AND LET GO

There's a new kind of passion I'm learning now, the passion to let go. Not of the mission. Not of the calling. Let go of control. Of the need to always be the one doing it all.

I've built things. I've turned organizations around. I've raised millions. I've grown teams from the ground up. Now I find myself in a season where my greatest impact is not what I build, but who I build. I don't need to be the hero in every story. I need to raise heroes who can write their own.

That's why I celebrate when someone I've coached takes the lead, when a young staffer stands up and owns the room. When a new voice enters the conversation with boldness. When one of my own kids begins to lead in their own way, not as my shadow, but as their own person. That's passion too. The kind that releases instead of controls.

And it's hard. Because passion wants to hold. It wants to protect. Love knows when to step back and let others rise.

FINDING PASSION AGAIN

There were seasons I thought I'd lost it. After my grandpa died, again when my son Nathaniel died, and of course when my late wife Laura passed away, after the chaos of transition, after betrayal and burnout, I wondered if the fire would come back. If I could ever love this work the same way. If I could still give without resentment. Still show up without fear.

Then I found myself laughing again. Worshipping again. Dreaming again. Writing again. The flame was still there, it just needed air. It needed space. It needed permission to be reborn, not recycled.

Passion doesn't always look the same. What once roared may now glow. What once shouted may now whisper. It's still holy. It's still powerful. It's still worth protecting.

"Never be lacking in zeal, but keep your spiritual fervor, serving the Lord." — Romans 12:11 (NIV)

I've returned to this verse again and again in every season of my leadership. It reminds me that passion isn't just emotional, it's spiritual. It's not something you drum up for appearances. It's something you protect. You don't lose passion because the work stops mattering. You lose it because you stop tending to what made it matter in the first place.

Staying passionate means staying connected. It means returning to your why when the how gets hard. It means serving with your whole heart, even when your heart has been broken. It means letting your work be worship, not because you're perfect, but because you're faithful.

LEADERSHIP LESSON: PASSION – RELATIONAL AND MISSION-FOCUSED

Passion is not volume. It's not hype. It's not just about being energized; it's about being anchored. It is the foundational fuel of a leader, but it must be focused, or it will lead you astray. Passionate leaders are those who remember the faces behind the mission. They lead with love, sacrifice comfort, and let their deepest convictions guide their decisions, not their convenience.

Here's the truth: passion without wisdom becomes recklessness. Passion without balance becomes burnout. That's why the greatest leaders are not the ones with the most energy, but the ones with the deepest emotional alignment to the purpose, the people, and the God who called them to it. None of the principles in this book work in isolation. We need passion balanced by discipline. We need initiative powered by passion. We need to be teachable as a disciplined part of how we lead.

I can be very passionate about everything, and my passion could overwhelm people. I have to set up systems and structures so that I don't send out every idea to everyone every time I think about something new. I call the list "Mike's Ideas" and the subtitle could be "things I don't have to accomplish right away." They are still important to me but I can't let them muddy the water.

If you have a lot of ideas, like I do, a lot of projects that may conflict and yet are all important, you can risk overwhelm for yourself and your team. That kind of overwhelm leads to burnout because it contains confusion around priorities. I find you have to set up systems and structure around the passion so you don't burden yourself or your team with all the ideas at once. So, I don't send every idea to everyone every time I think about it. I have a list just called "Mike's ideas," full of random thoughts. Once listed, I don't feel like I have to accomplish all of them right away. I stay focused on the real priorities.

Real passion doesn't make you the center of the universe, it teaches you to make room for others. For family. For friendship. For faith. Passion is powerful, but it's not eternal unless it's rooted in something bigger than you.

Passion must be protected, or it will die under the weight of your own expectations. When it's healthy, honest, and Spirit-filled, it changes lives. It keeps you going when everything around you says to quit. It helps others believe when they've stopped believing in themselves.

It stays.

It sees.

It saves.

REDISCOVERING, RECOVERING OR RE-ROUTING PASSION

People who can't find access to their passion are often numb or worn out or they have been in survival mode in their job for too long. It's probably not that passion is gone. It's just buried under exhaustion and disappointment. You don't have to chase it, you just need to clear enough space to feel it again. Passion doesn't have to be heavy. It doesn't have to be saving the world. If you're happy doing administration and you feel good about having a servant heart and helping other people, that's passion. If somebody enjoys selling cars and they care about what they're selling, that's passion.

People are chasing some idea of what passion is and comparing what they are doing to what other people are doing. You don't have to be envious of anyone else. What brings them alive may not do the same for you. Your passion comes alive when you feel good, when you're happy, when you're excited, when you love going to work, or love volunteering, or love doing what you're doing. If you are trying to follow someone else's passion and you are miserable, then you're probably making other people miserable, and you're probably not doing a good job.

Sometimes passion starts out quietly as curiosity or compassion, but it just doesn't go away. It's not always loud, and it can be subtle. You may not be as passionate about your job but you have found other things that feed your soul. You might volunteer, get on boards, get involved in agencies or churches, and feel passion that way.

We can re-route to our passion through exploring our curiosity. Sometimes what we find will cause us to make a change in our lives. I saw that happen during the economic crash in 2008. When the market crashed, I saw realtors and other business people who lost money in the market and realized that they weren't passionate about what they were doing. I followed them as they started applying for jobs in areas that fed their souls.

Don't look for passion through comparison or other outside ways to keep score. Look for passion in connection. Be around people who are alive with purpose. Passion is contagious. Ask questions, try things, serve someone, move toward people who remind you that your life still matters. Passion will meet you there.

RECALCULATING: THE FIRE THAT DOESN'T BURN OUT

Passion is what makes you stay when it would be easier to leave.

It's what drives you to care deeply when no one else seems to. It's not hype, it's heat. A slow, sustaining fire that keeps your heart engaged, even when your circumstances are draining you dry.

Passion must be protected. It must be focused. Because passion without direction leads to burnout. Passion without people turns into ego.

I've been there, when the mission became more about outcomes than hearts. When I lost sight of the "why" behind the "what." When I gave my best to the work and the scraps to the people I loved most.

But I've also found it again, through music, through ministry, through moments with my kids and my team, where I remembered: this is why I do it.

Passion is the compass that keeps your soul aligned. It's not the loudest part of you. It's the most honest. When you lead from that place, not performance, but purpose, people feel it.

They follow it.

They rise in it.

REFLECTION: FUEL YOUR FIRE WITHOUT BURNING OUT

Take time to reflect on these questions and let them guide you back to your center:

- What part of your leadership still sets your soul on fire? Are you giving it the time and energy it deserves—or are you letting busyness bury it?
- Have you started leading from performance instead of presence? Who around you needs to feel your passion relationally this week?
- What gift or voice have you silenced in the name of productivity? How could it be reawakened as part of your leadership again?
- When was the last time your leadership felt like worship? What would it look like to return to that rhythm?
- What would your team, your family, or your closest friends say you're most passionate about? Does it match what you want to be remembered for?

*Lead well.
Love deeper.

And never stop
learning.*

chapter five

LEADING
WITH LOVE AND KINDNESS

---

*"It's not what you say that people remember—
it's how you made them feel."*

THE LEADER WHO LEARNS TO LOVE HIMSELF

What if the hardest person to lead with love… is yourself?

It took me a long time to realize this: you can't truly lead with love if you don't believe you're worthy of love yourself.

I've always been the protector. The provider. The one who keeps pushing forward. Somewhere along the way, I lost sight of my own worth, not in God's eyes, not in the mission, but in my own. It's easy to love the work and forget to love yourself in it. Easy to speak life into others while quietly starving for it. When you've spent years proving yourself by overworking, over-delivering, over-carrying, it's hard to accept love that comes without strings attached.

There was a season when I didn't like who I saw in the mirror. Not because I had failed, but because I couldn't see the man behind the leadership anymore. I had gained weight. I had lost time with my family. I was still effective, still respected, but somewhere inside, I felt hollow.

That's when love started to teach me something new.

Love isn't just about being kind to others, it's about being kind to yourself. It's about letting grace take root in your own soul. It's about refusing to define your worth by your waistline, your résumé, or your performance. Love says, *"You're enough, even while you're still becoming."*

Leading with love starts there. You can't pour compassion from a cup filled with shame. You can't model kindness to your team if the voice in your own head is constantly cruel.

I had to start practicing what I preached. Eating healthier, not just for weight loss, but because I'm worth caring for. Saying no to things that drained me. Sitting with God without needing to perform. Letting rest become holy again.

It didn't make me weaker. It made me human. That humanity transformed my leadership more than any strategy ever could.

THE PEOPLE WHO CARRIED ME

For me, there were dozens.

There was the mentor who sat with me after Laura died and simply let me cry. The colleague who quietly stepped in during a meeting when I couldn't find the words. The staff member who handed me a handwritten card that said, *"You make this place feel like home."*

These weren't grand, performative gestures. They were small, sacred acts of love; real kindness in motion.

They reminded me: kindness doesn't always come from someone above you on the org chart. Sometimes it comes from the bottom up. Sometimes the very people you think you're leading are the ones keeping your spirit alive.

I've seen love show up in donuts and late-night texts, in whispered prayers behind closed doors, in teammates who refused to let me quit when everything in me said, *"I'm done."*

That's the kind of culture I want to build. Not just one where love is present, but one where love is practiced.

WHEN LOVE CONFRONTS, NOT CODDLES

Love calls you higher. It doesn't allow you to settle for mediocrity. It confronts what's broken because it believes you're worth more than your worst moment.

One of the kindest, yet most difficult, things I ever did as a leader was letting a staff member go.

It wasn't out of anger. It wasn't to make a statement. It was because I loved them enough to be honest with them. They were in the wrong role. They were drowning in it, and deep down, they knew it.

I didn't shame them. I didn't try to break them. Instead, I sat with them, acknowledged the reality we both saw, and helped them figure out the next right step. Not because I wanted to win, but because I truly wanted to love them through the process.

We don't have to blow up someone's life. We can realize that even when we part ways, even when there are huge mistakes, even when someone is not the right fit, we can still honor what they have done. When the church let me go, I wished they had honored the time we spent building something and let me know with love that it wasn't working for them anymore. You don't have to end a collaboration by email. You don't have to show up at someone's office door with a box. You don't have to cause anxiety, hopelessness, or pressure, you can find ways to make leaving or parting or ending kind, loving, and humane.

In my life, in work, love and kindness isn't always reciprocated, but it's important to stay strong even when love and kindness are not reflected back. Throughout my career, and in real time today, God does not show up in the ways I imagined, but in the end, God comes through, as he re-routes my life and opens other doors. That's the kind of leadership that's needed today. It's kindness that's unafraid of accountability. It's love that speaks the truth, not to punish, but to restore. Not to control, but to release.

The goal isn't perfection. It's wholeness.

LOVE THAT LIVES IN SYSTEMS

Love is present in how your team is structured, in who gets hired, who gets promoted, and who gets recognized. It shows up in your budget, in your training, and in how many chairs are at the table and who you're saving a seat for.

Love is about making your organization accessible, not just physically, but emotionally and culturally. It's about whether your strategy is just a brochure or a meaningful blueprint. It's about whether your financial assistance policy asks, "Prove you're worthy," or "Tell us how we can help."

I've sat in meetings where people wanted to cut programs deemed "underperforming," yet those same programs were feeding communities that no one else would serve. I've been with donors who questioned the value of certain initiatives because they couldn't see a return on investment in loving the least, the last, and the left out. I knew that is where love truly belongs.

I've walked into offices where the highest-paid leader had an office with a door and a nameplate, while the person cleaning the floors didn't even have their name on the schedule.

You want to lead with love? Start there. Ask yourself: *Who feels invisible here?* Then do something about it.

Kindness must be operationalized. You don't simply talk about culture, you build it, brick by brick, in the way people are treated when they mess up, when they speak up, when they grow, and even when they leave.

Love isn't just written in your mission statement. It's found in your meeting agendas. It's in who speaks, who listens, and how much room there is for both.

LOVE IN THE MIDDLE OF THE STORM

I'll never forget the moment one of my senior leaders came into my office and sat down, eyes glassy, shoulders slumped. They had been dealing with a personal crisis, something deep, raw, and ongoing and it had started affecting their work.

I could've launched into coaching mode. I could've reminded them of deadlines. I could've asked about progress reports. Something in me stopped. Instead, I just said, "How are you, *really?*"

The floodgates opened.

Not just tears, but relief. Because someone saw them. Not their title. Not their tasks. *Them.*

We talked. We paused deadlines. We created a plan. We reshaped their role so they could breathe again. They stayed. They thrived. Today, they're stronger and more loyal than ever, not because I handled them, but because I loved them.

That's the kind of leadership that changes lives. Not grand gestures. Presence. Empathy. Courage. Room to breathe.

CULTURE CHANGE IS A KINDNESS MOVEMENT

In several organizations I had the pleasure of leading, I inherited a culture that had forgotten how to trust. People were holding their breath, waiting for the next shift, the next change, the next letdown. You could feel it in the hallways, in the way people guarded their voices, held back ideas, and kept their hearts off the table.

I knew we couldn't rebuild the organization until we rebuilt belief.

So, we started slow. Not with strategy decks, but with story circles. With shout-outs in meetings. With intentional thank-yous, handwritten notes, surprise celebrations, moments of recognition that said, "I see you."

We shifted our hiring practices to focus on heart, not just history. We created policies that prioritized families, personal time, and mental health. We paid attention to people's stories, where they came from, what they carried, and what they needed to thrive. Guess what? Productivity went up. Turnover went down. The soul of the organization began to change, not because we demanded excellence, but because we nurtured it.

Even in the midst of re-structuring, building on this kindness, there are people behind the scenes who will resist every effort, they may even work harder against you, which is always a surprise. Yet, this is not a call to change my values or even my behavior. I know that leaders need to stay true to our values even when it does not work in our favor. That is the definition of integrity. I have stayed true to my values and continued with kindness and love anyway.

That's what kindness does. It's not extra. It's essential.

KINDNESS THAT REWRITES LEGACY

You don't get to choose how people remember every moment, but you do shape the story they tell about your leadership.

Years from now, no one will remember your budget projections. They won't recite your board reports. They won't name the specific metrics you hit. What they'll remember is the moment they sat in your office with their head down, thinking their job or their worth was on the line, and you looked them in the eye and said, "You're not alone."

They'll remember the leader who didn't raise their voice, even when they could've. The one who invited them back into the room after a failure. The one who made space for their grief, their growth, and their process, not just their performance.

I've seen what happens when leaders choose control over compassion. I've watched organizations lose their best people because someone couldn't admit they were wrong. I've seen brilliance walk out the door because love wasn't the operating system; it was just a speech on the wall.

I've also seen what happens when a leader takes the time to listen. When someone gets promoted not because they were perfect, but because they were passionate. When a culture begins to heal because kindness is no longer treated like fluff, but like fire.

You want to change the legacy of your leadership? Start here: What does love look like in how you lead when no one's watching?

THE GRACE TO GROW

There was a time when a young leader on my team made a major mistake; something public, costly, and deeply emotional. They were devastated. Ready to resign. Truthfully, part of me wanted to let them.

I paused. I remembered my own journey; the moments I messed up and someone chose grace instead of dismissal. The times I failed, and someone believed in me anyway.

So I brought them into my office, closed the door, and said something I think more leaders need to say: *"This was real. It was wrong. It's not the end. Let's grow from this."*

We talked. We cried. We rebuilt. And that leader? They stayed. They matured. They've never made the same mistake again, not because I shamed them, but because I reminded them they were still worth investing in.

You want people to grow? Don't just correct them. Cover them. Not to hide the truth, but to hold space for transformation.

That's what love does. It doesn't coddle. It covers. It doesn't excuse. It equips. It says, *"I'll sit with you in the mess, but I won't leave you here."*

LOVE THAT OUTLASTS YOU

One day, I won't be the leader. I won't be the one with the keys, the office, or the calendar full of meetings. I hope long after I've passed the baton there will be people who still walk the hallways saying, "He believed in me." Not because I had to, because I chose to.

That's legacy.

Legacy isn't how big your title got. It's how deeply your love reached.

It's in the intern you stopped to mentor. The staff member you pulled aside after a hard day. The volunteer you spoke life into when they were about to give up. The teammate you forgave because you saw the pain under their pride.

Titles fade. Structures change. Strategies shift.

But love? Love sticks. Love gets remembered. Love outlasts you.

"Let all that you do be done in love." — 1 Corinthians 16:14 (ESV)

Not some of what you do. Not just what feels convenient. Not only what earns applause. *All* of it.

The conversations. The corrections. The hires. The fires. The visions. The revisions. Let it all be done in love.

Love isn't weakness. It's not secondary to success. It's not the cherry on top of performance. It's the foundation. The engine. The invitation to lead in a way that leaves people better, not just more productive.

If God's greatest command is love, then your greatest leadership strategy should be the same.

RECALCULATING: LOVE AND KINDNESS ARE YOUR GREATEST INFLUENCE

They move people. They shape cultures. They leave legacies. They are the reason people follow you long after the paycheck, the project, or the position has faded.

To lead with love means putting people first, not titles or tasks. It means choosing dignity over domination, grace over shame, and clarity over fear.

> *"I have fought the good fight, I have finished the race, I have kept the* **FAITH.***"*

– 2 TIMOTHY 4:7

It means understanding that accountability is most effective when it's rooted in empathy, not ego.

To lead with kindness means showing up with presence, not performance. It means remembering names, forgiving failures, creating safety, and offering correction with care. It means seeing the invisible, celebrating the overlooked, and building a culture where people truly believe they matter.

Kindness is not weakness. Love is not a distraction. They are the deepest, most transformative strategies in the world.

The kind that makes people want to stay. The kind that restores teams instead of replacing them. The kind that opens doors you could never kick down with skill alone.

Because in the end, **love wins. Always.**

REFLECTION: LOVE THAT LEADS

Take a moment to reflect on the love that shaped you and the love you now offer others.

- Who showed you love and kindness when you least deserved it? How did it change your story?
- What are some small ways you can build systems of kindness into your team or organization?
- Are you making time for love in your leadership, or just results?
- Where have you held back kindness in the name of "standards"? Is it time to revisit your approach?
- What would it look like to lead with so much love that people **felt** it long after they stopped working with you?

When the spotlight fades, because it always does,

let your legacy speak louder than your résumé ever could.

THE RE-ROUTE THAT CHANGED EVERYTHING

If you've made it this far, you've walked through valleys with me. You've stood in boardrooms and hospital rooms. You've felt the weight of leadership and the ache of loss. You've learned the four principles that have shaped my leadership: Teachability, Initiative, Discipline, and Passion. This book wouldn't be complete if I didn't tell you about what's happened since the "re-routing" that brought me to Texas. Because the truth is God wasn't done. Not even close.

Five years ago, I moved to Fort Worth to take a job. I didn't know that what I was really stepping into was healing, redemption, and restoration on a scale I could've never imagined. I didn't know that God would re-route me once again, and that I would be looking in the mirror to find my value, not to the outside world. I did not know I would learn that I could maintain my kindness and love even when they were challenged by the very people I trusted. Fort Worth is my home and what God has presented gives me hope and inspiration that I can and will accomplish my life goals, including this book, my family consulting business and the ability to support people across the entire world. This chapter isn't about starting over, but what happens when God finally brings you full circle.

A NEW LOVE, A NEW BEGINNING

When I met Stacy, I wasn't looking to rebuild. My heart was still grieving. I had buried my wife, Laura, and our infant son, Nathaniel. I had said goodbye to a version of life I thought would last forever. Grief, as painful as it is, makes room. In that space, love surprised me again.

My daughter and my mother were the ones who said, "Hey, it's time that you should think about starting to date." They introduced me to online dating. My daughter ran the app and the process. Stacy was the first or second person I talked to and got to know. What got my attention was that she was interested in who my late wife was, in our family, and in the context of my life, even on the first date. She had that heart of gold. We also had similar interests, loved spending time together, but she was never trying to fill Laura's place. She is a sweet, kind, humble person who cares deeply about our whole large, blended family.

As a later-in-life, second marriage for us, we have also learned that communication is key. Honesty is key. We need to be able to talk about anything. We get to spend more time together in a less stressful way. We don't have three-year-olds running around, we are not in the building phase of a young family so we get to do it differently. Our challenge has been bringing together our two individual families into one whole. It hasn't always been easy. Even my daughter, who ran my dating process, has had to come to accept that Stacy is not here to take her mother's place. We had some rocky moments about Stacy making the house hers also. There was a battle over soap dispensers which stood in for a whole lot of feelings. Stacy's compassion made it all work.

Stacy came into my life not as a replacement but as a reminder that there is life after loss, joy after sorrow, and purpose even when your plans are shattered. Her two sons, Wyatt and Hayden, didn't just become part of my story, they became part of my heart. We became a blended family, not perfect but powerful. Each of us carried our pasts, our pain, and our hopes for the future, trying to make something beautiful out of all the broken.

And somehow… we did.

THE KIDS WHO BECAME MY LEGACY

Each of our six kids has taken their path, and none of them has made it easy, but they've made it meaningful. My daughter Abbie went off to college to chase her dreams, working summers at the Y like her dad once did. Colby and his best friend Danny are building their own business, putting vision into motion. Hayden, Stacy's oldest, earned his master's degree and is now a thriving leader, proving that character will always outshine credentials. Wyatt, the youngest, came home from college and is leaning into health and fitness, discovering his strength in Christ and himself.

Then there are my oldest boys, Robbie and Kevin. They came back to Fort Worth. Back to me. Back to grace. Robbie is over two years sober, working through his past and making steps I used to pray for in silence. Kevin, too, is facing his own decisions, and he's here and present, trying, moving forward. They're not the identical boys I adopted years ago. They're men now. Though their paths haven't been easy, their progress is holy. Healing takes time. They're still walking. That's what matters.

A FAMILY FINALLY TOGETHER

As if all of that weren't enough, something I never thought possible happened. My mom, my 97-year-old grandmother, my sister Mandi, and her three kids all moved to Fort Worth. They bought homes. They put down roots. For the first time in over 35 years, almost all of my family lives in one place. My dad and some extended family are still in California, but my heart has never felt more gathered.

Do you know what seeing all your generations in one room is like? To watch your kids laugh with their cousins? To know that you don't have to fly across the country to share a meal with your mom or help your grandma with groceries? It's sacred. It's stretching, too but don't get me wrong. Four people still live at home. Time is tight. Demands are high. I've prayed for these problems. I've begged God for a season where the challenge was choosing between good things, not surviving the bad ones.

It's not perfect, things rarely are. In the imperfection we are still figuring out how to put the past behind us, but deep down, regardless of anything, I believe love will show up and the future with family back in my life will become one of the greatest chapters in my life story.

THE HARDEST GOODBYE, THE HOLIEST GROUND

One of the most sacred moments of this new season was finally placing Laura, Nathaniel, and our nineteen-year-old cat's ashes in one urn and giving them a resting place right here in Fort Worth, fifteen minutes from home, a place we can visit, remember, and honor. It wasn't easy. Emotionally, I wrestled with timing and guilt. Stacy was there, holding me up and reminding me that love doesn't expire. It expands.

Now, when I drive past that cemetery, I don't just feel sadness. I feel peace. I feel complete. The story didn't end, it just turned the page.

STILL LEARNING, STILL LEADING

If you're reading this book expecting a neat bow on top, I must be honest. I'm still learning how to do this, still figuring out how to balance leadership and love, purpose and presence, family and future. There are days I get it right, and days I don't. There are relationships I still need to repair, time I still need to reclaim, and emotions I still need to unpack.

Here's the good news: I'm not alone. I have Stacy. I have my kids. I have friends that believe in my life vision. I have a family that finally feels close. I have a God who keeps rerouting me, not because I'm lost, but because He's leading me deeper.

The organization I once led in Fort Worth is moving forward. That culture is transforming. Our reach has expanded. The mission has never felt more alive. A small part of me hopes I made some sort of difference. None of that compares to the legacy I'm building at home. The dinners. The laughs. The coaching talks with my kids. The tears that are shared behind closed doors. The new traditions we're making. That's the real re-route. That's a miracle.

LOVE, KINDNESS, AND WHAT COMES NEXT

So what's next? Honestly, I'm not sure. I do know this: I want to live the rest of my life pouring love and kindness like never before. I want to show up fully for my family, my friends, my community, and the God who's never left my side. I want to tell leaders that titles mean nothing without integrity, strategy without presence, and leadership means nothing if it doesn't come from love.

This story, my story, is still being written. If you've walked through this book with me, if you've seen your reflection in my pain or your hope in my healing, then let this final chapter remind you of something powerful:

You are never too far gone. Never too old to start again. Never too broken to be used. Never too wounded to lead with strength. Never too late to be re-routed.

Because sometimes the best chapters come after you thought the story was over.

WHEN THE SPOTLIGHT FADES, THIS IS WHAT REMAINS

There's a truth most leaders won't say out loud: you can know all the right things and still miss your moment. You can have read every leadership book on the shelf and still collapse when pressure hits. Because knowing isn't doing. Without these principles forming the structure of your character, pressure will always expose your foundation.

I've seen it firsthand in myself and others. Early in my career, I had to learn that being **teachable** wasn't just about listening during a workshop.

It meant swallowing my pride when I thought I was right. It meant hearing "you need to slow down" when I wanted to speed up. It meant learning to say, "I was wrong" even when every part of me wanted to justify, deflect, or defend.

Here's the thing about teachability: it often doesn't feel like growth at first. It feels like humbling. It feels like sitting in someone else's office with your stomach in knots because you didn't get it right. It feels like that internal wrestle between old patterns and new potential. If you stick with it, you realize that teachability isn't about what you know. **Teachability is about who you're becoming.**

Initiative? That one's personal, too. I didn't build a career by being the most polished or pedigreed. I didn't grow through waiting for promotions or asking for permission. I showed up early, asked how I could help, and said yes to the jobs no one else wanted. I filled the gap.

In Georgia, we didn't have a roadmap, we had a blank canvas. Initiative became the brush in my hand. Whether it was launching a youth program, organizing worship nights, or driving across town to connect with kids who were slipping through the cracks, the work didn't get done because it was easy, it got done because I couldn't wait for someone else to do it.

Initiative looks like looking around and thinking, *This matters too much for me to wait.*

And **discipline?** It wasn't glamorous. But it saved me.

Discipline was staying up late at night to finish a staff evaluation, even when my heart was breaking. It was showing up for morning meetings after holding Laura through the night. It was making decisions I didn't feel strong enough to make, but doing them anyway because other people were counting on me.

Discipline is what kept me upright when grief threatened to level me. **Discipline is what made me dependable even when my life felt undependable.**

And **passion?** Passion is the part of me that never left even when I wanted to or questioned my calling. When I lost my wife. When I watched my kids cry in silence, I couldn't fix it. Passion was the flame God kept alive when everything inside me burned out. **Passion reminded me that this life is still worth building, that people are still worth believing in, that purpose doesn't disappear when you're in pain, it deepens.**

That's what these principles are: **your survival kit for calling.**

They're not for when everything is going right. They're for the storm.

They're what keep your feet planted when the wind kicks up.

They give you something to hold on to when the applause dies down and the room gets quiet and you're left alone with your doubt.

They're not the exciting part of leadership.

They're the essential part.

Because at the end of the day, when the role changes, when the seasons shift, when you're no longer the one everyone is looking to, these things will have built a life, not just a résumé.

These are the habits that hold you when the spotlight goes off.

These are the values that make you someone worth following.

When you live this calling, you leave a legacy behind. You leave a legacy of new, inspired leaders in your wake. Leadership is not about what you have accumulated when all is said and done. It's not about how many programs you launched or how many campuses bore your name. It's not about the titles you held, the stages you spoke on, or the budgets you managed. Leadership, authentic, enduring leadership is about people. It's about presence. It's about whether, in your wake, someone else stood taller, walked straighter, and believed deeper because you saw them. Because you poured into them. Because your life whispered, "You matter."

You whispered "You matter," through your teachability, initiative, discipline, and passion.

People think legacy is about the person. It's not. Legacy is about the process. It's not even about a "successful" process. All of us have failures. Those failures do not impact the growth in the people, system, and structure you created daily through your love, teachability, discipline, initiative, and passion. The legacy is simple. It's not about me, but the culture I created and the changes that were made to how people lead. If people are living out those principles, it is a gift.

See, legacy isn't something you leave behind when you die. It's something you live with now. Every interaction, decision, and act of humility or encouragement becomes part of the soil someone else grows in. If we're honest, most of us won't be remembered for our greatest achievements. We will be remembered for how we made people feel. For how we led when it was hard. Whether we protected our values when it would've been easier to cut corners. For how many people we lifted when they felt forgotten.

"*We will tell the next generation the praiseworthy deeds of the* LORD..."

— PSALM 78:4

LIFELINES

The funny thing about leadership is that it rarely looks like how you imagined it when you first signed up. You think it's going to be strategy, vision, and change-making. Sometimes, it is. More often? It's the quiet sacrifices no one sees. It's holding space for someone else's pain while hiding your own. It's fighting for culture when cynicism would be easier.

That's when these principles stop being ideas and become lifelines.

I think about the nights I drove home from board meetings feeling like I had nothing left in the tank. I think about the stretch in Rockford where it felt like every conversation was uphill. I was trying to cast a vision in a place that didn't want to see it. Trying to stir momentum where survival had become the norm.

I remember the day one of my team members, burned out and bitter, looked me in the eyes and said, "Why even try?"

They weren't talking about the work. They were talking about *hope*.

That's when you realize this leadership thing was never about being the smartest or the most strategic. It was about being **the one who keeps believing** when belief is in short supply.

That's what passion does.

It doesn't just ignite you, it sustains others.

I didn't feel particularly powerful in that moment. I did what I've trained myself to do when I have nothing else: I showed up. I stayed steady. I leaned into the pain instead of away from it. Little by little, that team member came back to life. Not because I had the perfect answer, but because I refused to stop showing up with heart.

THESE PRINCIPLES ARE NOT INTERCHANGEABLE. THEY'RE INTERDEPENDENT.

You can't have passion without discipline. It'll burn out.

You can't have initiative without teachability. It'll go off course.

You can't have discipline without passion. It'll turn robotic.

And you can't be teachable without initiative. You'll just sit on wisdom instead of using it.

They support each other. When one feels weak, the others reinforce it. Over time, they form something stronger than hype or charisma: they form **character**.

And character is what lasts.

It's what builds trust over time. It's what makes people feel safe following you. It's what helps you sleep at night, not because everything went perfectly, but because you know you led with consistency, conviction, and care.

These four principles don't just make you a leader.

They make you someone people want to build with, someone they believe in, and someone they know will still be standing when the storm passes.

That's the kind of leader I want to be.

Not flashy. Not flawless. **Faithful.**

*"**Whatever you do, work at it with all your heart, as working for the Lord, not for human matters.**" — **Colossians 3:23 (NIV)***

This is the heart of it all.

These four principles: **Teachability, Initiative, Discipline,** and **Passion** aren't just leadership hacks. They're the essence of **whole-hearted living**. The world doesn't need more impressive leaders, it needs more *anchored* ones. Leaders who work not for applause, but for purpose. Not for image, but for impact. Leaders who know that every meeting, every decision, every act of care is an offering. A way of saying: *This matters because they matter. Because he matters.*

Leadership is sacred. Build it on what lasts.

THE END, THAT BECAME THE NEW BEGINNING

Sometimes the re-route is unexpected. Most of the time, I don't fully understand what God is doing until I look back and realize He was preparing me long before I felt ready. I have learned that you can give your entire life to meaningful work, lead with passion and discipline, stay teachable, and still find yourself standing at the edge of something new without a clear map in hand. That moment does not mean you failed. It usually means you are being invited forward.

As I wrote this book, something surprising happened. Instead of draining me, it brought me alive. Telling the truth about my story, my leadership, my faith, and my losses didn't close chapters for me, it opened them. It reminded me that I am still curious. Still growing. Still willing to be shaped. Writing these pages did not pull me backward. It clarified who I am becoming.

There was a time when I believed that strong leadership meant certainty. Clear plans. Defined outcomes. Confidence that never wavered. Life has corrected that assumption. Strength, I now know, often looks like openness. Like humility. Like the willingness to step into the unknown with faith instead of fear. This season of change in my work and calling did not come with a dramatic announcement or a perfectly scripted transition. It came quietly, gradually, and with a growing sense of peace that told me it was time to move differently.

After more than thirty-five years of leading in community, I am not walking away from purpose. I am walking deeper into it. I am discovering new ways to serve leaders, organizations, and missions that matter. Coaching. Consulting. Philanthropic development. Encouraging others to lead with heart, clarity, and courage. This work feels both new and familiar, like a continuation rather than a departure. The same values guide me. The same love for people fuels me. Only the setting has changed.

Change has also been happening closer to home, reminding me that family is not one clean narrative, but a collection of relationships shaped by love, history, grief, and time. My wife and children anchor me in the present and invite me to keep choosing joy and forward motion. My in-laws, including Laura's parents, remain my family still, bound by a love that did not end with loss and continues to teach me what faithfulness looks like over decades. At the same time, my relationship with my mom, my sister, and my grandmother continues to shape me in quieter, harder ways. These are bonds filled with deep love, shared history, and unresolved tension that does not disappear simply because we wish it would. They remind me that some relationships form us through closeness, others through distance, and all of them through truth.

While writing this book, I returned to Baltimore to stand with family as we laid Pop Pop to rest, a man named Wyatt whose life reflected steadiness, humility, and presence. His name carries sacred weight in my story, shared with my son, Nathaniel Wyatt Brown, whose brief life forever shaped my heart. In these moments, I am reminded that family is everything, even when it is imperfect, even when it is unfinished. As a leader, a husband, a father, a son, and a grandson, I am learning that I cannot control outcomes, only posture. I can choose grace without denial, hope without pressure, and love without conditions, trusting that what is still shaping us is not wasted, and that healing often works quietly, over time.

What gives me confidence in this season is not certainty about the future. It is confidence in the process. I have lived long enough now to know that re-routing is not interruption. It is invitation. God has never wasted my pain. He has never abandoned me in transition. He has never asked me to stop loving, stop leading, or stop believing. He has only asked me to keep walking.

I am more at peace now than I have been in years. Not because life is easier, but because I am more aligned. I am less concerned with proving myself and more committed to being present. Less attached to titles and more invested in impact. Less afraid of change and more open to what it produces in me.

If there is one thing I hope you take from this book, it is this. Your life does not need to make sense to be meaningful. Your leadership does not need to be perfect to be powerful. And your next chapter does not need to look like your last one to be faithful. Sometimes the bravest thing you can do is release what was good so you can receive what is next.

I am embracing life again. Fully. Honestly. With gratitude for where I have been and excitement for where I am going. I do not know all the details, but I know the direction. Forward. With love. With purpose. With people.

This book does not end with closure. It ends with momentum. With curiosity. With hope. With a man who has learned that re-routing is not a detour from life, but one of the ways life grows us into who we were always meant to become.

This is not an ending defined by loss.

It is a beginning shaped by wisdom.

And I am walking into it with open hands.

REFLECTION: A LEADERSHIP INVENTORY

Take a breath. Be honest with yourself. Let these questions pull something deeper out of you.

- **Teachability** – Where have you stopped learning because you feel like you've "arrived"? What could change if you got curious again?
- **Initiative** – Where are you waiting for permission when you've already been equipped? What's one bold move you've been hesitating on?
- **Discipline** – Which area of your life feels chaotic right now? What daily rhythm or boundary could restore order?
- **Passion** – What part of your leadership still lights you up? Have you been neglecting it? What would it look like to protect and prioritize it again?
- **Legacy** – Which of these four principles needs the most attention in your leadership today? What will your team, your family, or your community remember you for?

This is not just a leadership book.

It's a love letter to resilience.

A PERSONAL LETTER FROM MIKE BROWN, JR.

To the reader who made it all the way here, thank you. Not just for turning the pages, but for turning toward your growth. Thank you for opening your heart, reflecting deeply, and choosing to keep showing up as a leader even when it's hard, messy, and unglamorous. I don't take that lightly.

I didn't write this book to prove anything. I wrote it because I've lived through some things, real things. These are the kinds of things that don't always make it onto LinkedIn or conference keynotes. I've experienced wins and failures, heartbreak and healing, breakdowns and breakthroughs. I've led when I was strong, and I've led when I was barely holding it together. In every chapter of my life, I've come back to the same truth: you don't have to be perfect to be powerful. You don't have to have it all figured out to make a difference. You have to care enough to keep showing up with heart.

This book was born in the trenches. It came from hospital hallways and empty boardrooms, whispering desperate prayers in the middle of the night, standing at the grave of my son and still believing that God had more for me, watching one family fall apart. Another slowly come together in ways I never imagined possible, and mentoring emerging leaders who reminded me that leadership isn't about having the answers, it's about being present.

I've learned how to lead through loss, to rise again after failure, to sit in rooms where I felt judged and still speak with kindness. I've made painful mistakes. I've let my ego get in the way. I've lost friends I wish I had kept. I've missed moments with family, and I'll never get them back. I've parted from jobs I loved. I've walked out of meetings ashamed of how I showed up. Yet, through it all, love and kindness have always called me back. Always pointed me home.

If there's anything I want you to take away from this book, it's that leadership is not about your platform. It's about your posture. It's about who you are when the mic is off, the room is empty, and your integrity is the only thing you're left with. It's about whether the people who work for you and with you also feel like you see them. It's about whether your children, your friends, your coworkers, your neighbors, and your volunteers know what it's like to be led by someone who genuinely gives a damn.

You don't have to lead an organization to lead a legacy. You just have to lead one moment at a time; with love, purpose, and the kind of compassion that doesn't need applause to be powerful.

If you're reading this and wondering whether you're doing enough, let me encourage you; you are. If you've been leading through grief, burnout, confusion, or transition, you're not behind. If you've made some mistakes and wondered if it disqualifies you, take a breath. You're still in the game. You are not too far gone to lead with heart. In fact, that crack in your confidence might just be the doorway where grace enters.

I hope this book has become more than an inspiration. I hope it's become a mirror; a chance to see the best of who you already are and the next version of who you're becoming. A leader who is grounded in teachability, driven by initiative, anchored in discipline, and fueled by passion. A leader whose story won't be remembered for a title, but for transformation.

Don't just carry my story. Go write your own. Start where you are. Build something that outlives you. Invest in the people no one is watching. Give second chances, as if your life depends on it. Sit with the hurting. Cheer for the underdog. And never forget: your legacy doesn't begin when you retire. It starts with every decision you make today.

I'm proud of you. I believe in you. I can't wait to see what you build.

With heart,
Mike Brown, Jr.

STAY IN TOUCH

Visit the author at mikebrownjr.com to learn about his current projects, watch videos, join his mailing list, and more.